AN INTRODUCTION TO VASTU

AN INTRODUCTION TO VASTU

the Hindu tradition of arranging your
home to improve health and wellbeing

JONATHAN DEE

Published by SILVERDALE BOOKS
An imprint of Bookmart Ltd
Registered number 2372865
Trading as Bookmart Ltd
Desford Road
Enderby
Leicester LE19 4AD

© 2002 D&S Books Ltd

D&S Books Ltd
Kerswell
Parkham Ash
Devon, England
EX39 5PR

e-mail us at:-
enquiries@dsbooks.fsnet.co.uk

This edition printed 2002

ISBN 1-856056-77-5

All rights reserved. This book is protected by copyright. No part of it may be reproduced, stored in a retrieval system, or transmitted in any form or by any means, without the prior permission in writing of the Publisher, nor be circulated in any form of binding or cover other than that in which it is published and without a similar condition including this condition being imposed on the subsequent Publisher

Creative Director: Sarah King
Editor: Anna Southgate
Project editor: Sarah Harris
Photographer: Paul Forrester
Designer: Dave Jones

Typeset in Lithos and Avenir

Printed in China

1 3 5 7 9 10 8 6 4 2

CONTENTS

WHAT IS VASTU? 06
THE COSMIC SQUARE. 08
THE THREE FORCES 14
THE FIVE ELEMENTS. 20
THE DOMESTIC ZODIAC 26
PLANETARY PLACEMENTS 30
THE REGENTS OF SPACE. 38
APPLYING VASTU 46
THE ENTRANCE TO YOUR HOME . . . 60
THE LIVING ROOM 66
THE DINING AREA. 76
THE KITCHEN. 82
BEDROOMS 88
THE BATHROOM. 98
THE HOME OFFICE 104
INDEX 110
BIBLIOGRAPHY, CREDITS 112

WHAT IS VASTU?

OVER RECENT YEARS, we in the Western world have become accustomed to cultural concepts from other nations. One of the most notable of these is the Chinese art of feng shui, which proposes that the universe is filled with a life-giving force known as *chi*. According to this Oriental discipline our homes, and the way we arrange our furniture and possessions within them, can have a direct bearing on our health, wealth and general happiness.

Vastu is concerned with the correct use of space within a living area.

Simplicity and lack of clutter are desirable in both Feng Shui and Vastu.

However *feng shui* is not the only such cult to emerge from the Orient. Another, more ancient, culture also developed a variation on the art of placement. Originating in India, probably in prehistoric times, this discipline – only now coming to light in the West – is known as *Vastu Shastra*. The word *vastu* (pronounced vaastu) literally means 'dwelling', while *shastra* implies 'science' or 'knowledge'. Together they embody a method of harmonising the architectural design of a building with the placement of objects within it for the maximum benefit of its inhabitants. As with *feng shui*, Vastu also maintains that there is one, universal, animating force and this "breath of life" is known as *prana*. Vastu's similarity to *feng shui* should not come as a surprise since the latter is in fact a descendant of the Indian original, with the "science of placement" most likely entering China with the first Buddhist missionaries of the 3rd or 4th centuries BC.

WHAT IS VASTU?

The correct placement of furniture creates an atmosphere of calm serenity.

Among the teachings of Vastu, the ancient gods that feature in the holy texts known as the *Vedas* are deeply significant. However, this does not mean that one has to convert to Hinduism in order to practise Vastu. These gods – known as "regents of space" – are also symbols of cosmic forces and can be thought of as abstract principles rather than beings if preferred (see pages 38-45).

The defining message of *Vastu Shastra* is that, if we consciously mould our environment to reflect the positive vibrations of the universe, our souls and our physical selves will exist in harmony with the cosmos and we will be happier, more rounded and successful individuals.

Hindu temples are designed according to the principles of Vastu Shastra.

According to the teachings of Vastu, a correctly orientated living space, and the placement of the possessions within it, will grant serenity and security to those who spend time within it. Vastu promises to create a spiritual harmony as well as contributing to physical wellbeing and prosperity. In its original form *Vastu Shastra* is extremely complex, applying not only to internal living spaces, but also to gardens, building-plot developments – even the exact proportions of Hindu temples. The application of Vastu guidelines to the home is not difficult and, in this book, you will find simple ways of selecting a room for a specific purpose as well as tips for interior design and techniques for attracting positive *prana* into your home and your life.

THE COSMIC SQUARE

SAKALA, THE SQUARE, is the most potently symbolic shape in the Vastu system of the universe. The entire cosmos is imagined to be square in shape, with sides, corners and cardinal

Sunrise is connected to youthfulness, exuberance and new life in Vastu.

The heat of the South is arid and provides one extreme of the "Fire-Line".

points. This "cosmic square" is thought to unite two primary pairs of opposites – east and west (the directions of sunrise and sunset), and north and south (the directions of cold and heat). The directional points between these absolutes – northeast, southeast, southwest and northwest – express the various interrelationships between heat, beginnings, cold and endings.

Dusk is at the western end of the "Water Line" and is associated with endings.

Northern cold is at the "polar" extreme of the Agni-Rekha or Fire Line.

THE COSMIC SQUARE

To find the Fire, Water and Wind lines in your home you'll need to employ and ordinary magnetic compass to find the directions.

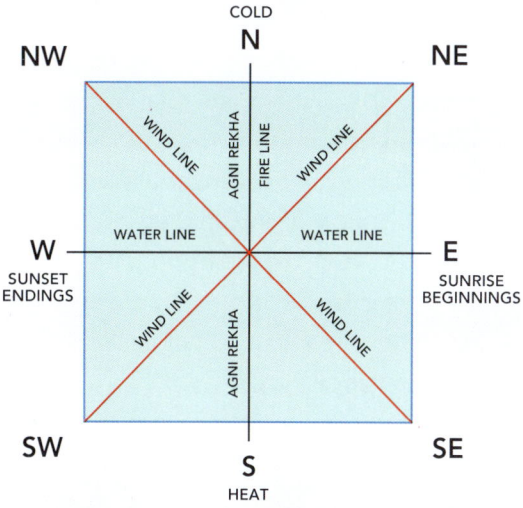

The lines within the square.

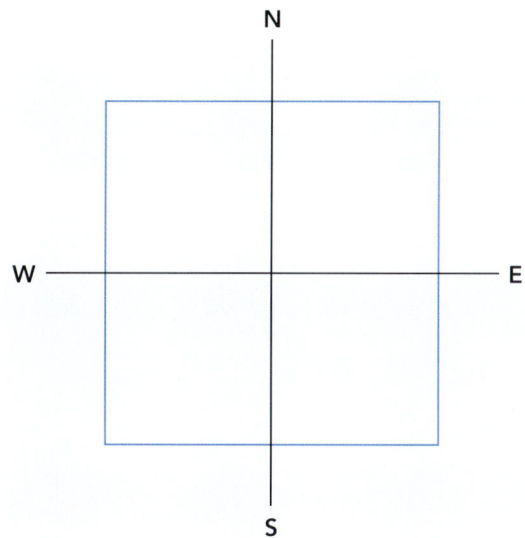

Each of the points, lines, corners, sides and directions of the cosmic square is symbolised by a god of the early Hindu faith, collectively known as the regents of space. Their various characters, associations and mythology serve to give clues as to the nature of the energies that come from the respective directions (see pages 38-45).

The many heads and arms of Hindu deities such as this symbolise the harmony of forces in the universe.

The north-south line through the centre of the cosmic square is called the *agni-rekha* or "fire line" and represents the backbone of the universe. The corresponding line running from east to west is called the "water line" and signifies that creative force flows along its length. Lines going from corner to corner are called "wind lines" and are associated with energy and dynamic movement. Combined, these interacting forces form a universal motivating force, *brahman* – the breath of the creator god Brahma.

AN INTRODUCTION TO VASTU

Any space that is square in shape will share Vastu principles. The home, whether a house or an apartment, is made up of squares and rectangles of varying sizes and so the Vastu guidelines can be applied with very little trouble. The cosmic square can be fitted into all living areas even those that happen to be 'L-shaped'. Simply divide an area into a series of squares and treat each according to the Vastu rules. Alternatively the largest of the squares can be lengthened, mentally, into a rectangle and the Vastu rules applied to this new area.

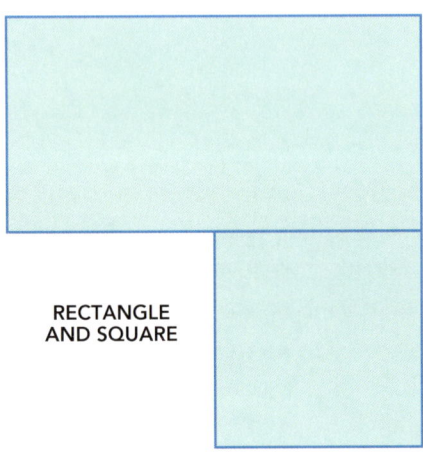

An 'L' shaped dwelling.

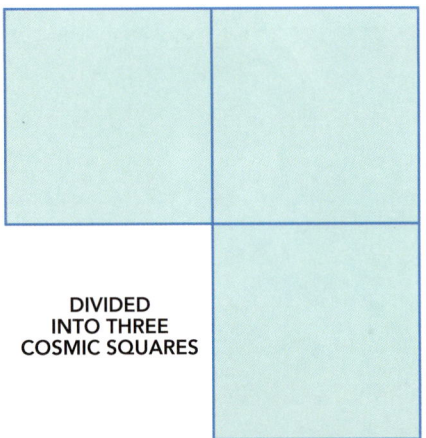

DIVIDING THE COSMIC SQUARE

We have already seen that the cosmic square has a star-like set of divisions from north to south, east to west and from corner to corner. There is also a more complex division based on numbers.

All forms of Eastern mysticism derive a significant proportion of their symbolism from numerology or the occult significance of everyday numbers. You will see that, in Vastu, there are three universal forces, five elements and seven planets (although with the addition of the shadow planets there are nine). There are also nine regents of space and twelve signs of the zodiac. Each of these values is expressed within the cosmic square as shown in the following diagram.

1	2	3	4	5	6	7	8	9
2	4	6	8	10	12	14	16	18
3	6	9	12	15	18	21	24	27
4	8	12	16	20	24	28	32	36
5	10	15	20	25	30	35	40	45
6	12	18	24	30	36	42	48	54
7	14	21	28	35	42	49	56	63
8	16	24	32	40	48	56	64	72
9	18	27	36	45	54	63	72	81

Calculations for the cosmic square.

This square is a visual representation of the nine times table, the highest number being nine times nine, eighty-one.

THE COSMIC SQUARE

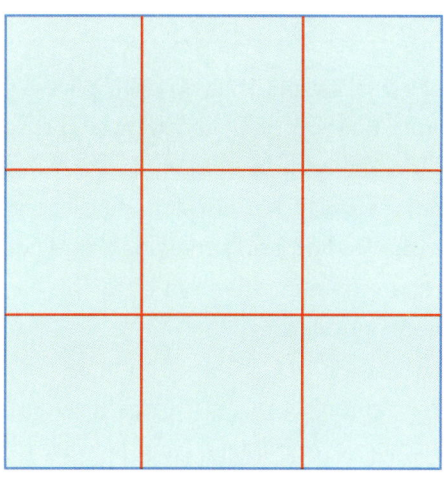

1	2	3	4	5	6	7	8	9
2	4	6	8	1	3	5	7	9
3	6	9	3	6	9	3	6	9
4	8	3	7	2	6	1	5	9
5	1	6	2	7	3	8	4	9
6	3	9	6	3	9	6	3	9
7	5	3	1	8	6	4	2	9
8	7	6	5	4	3	2	1	9
9	9	9	9	9	9	9	9	9

The Vedic Square.

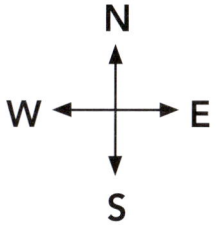

The cosmic square can also be expressed as the Vedic diagram in the following manner. Superimposed over any given area, this square is used to calculate the proportion of space that is influenced by any given direction, planet, zodiac sign or regent. In short, it is used to assess which part of a room or house 'belongs' to the northeast, southwest, and so on.

The Vedic Square in nine sections.

The Vedic diagram is used to show the precise divisions of any square-shaped living space. Traditionally, the "sacred centre" of this square is left unoccupied because it is considered to be the heart of the home, and the dwelling place of Brahma, the creator god, himself. This final diagram is a vital key to creating harmony in interior spaces.

A Hindu deity making and offering to the sacred principle of fire, Agni.

Red is emblematic of the creator god Brahma and is associated with the centre of anything.

11

AN INTRODUCTION TO VASTU

THE COSMIC SQUARE AND THE BODY

The correct application of Vastu principles is said to have a direct bearing on both physical and spiritual health. In India, the Vedic diagram is often visualised as a map of the body. More specifically, it represents the body of a demon and serves as a reminder that negative energies within the home may be harmful if they are not controlled.

This 'home demon' is called the *vastu purusha*. It is said to reside in every house, lying face down along the northeast-southwest wind line. Its head is located at the "gateway of the gods" (see page 19) while his feet occupy the negative southwest quarter.

The great gods of Hinduism battled a formless monster who threatened the earth.

THE TALE OF PURUSHA

The story of *vastu purusha* is founded in early Hindu mythology. According to legend there was once a huge demon that lacked a name or stable form. So vast was this sinister being that its bulk occupied the earth in every direction and its shadow blocked out the light of the sky. The gods became alarmed and joined together to seize the creature and force it down to the ground, pressing its face into the earth.

Once this was accomplished, the creator god Brahma enclosed the demon within a square to give it form. He granted it the name of Purusha and, in order to stop the demon moving, Brahma sat on its centre. He then chose eight of the most powerful deities to sit on the monster's other extremities, so preventing the demon ever escaping captivity.

The subdued monster, called Purusha was forced to the earth.

Brahma then said that terrible misfortune would occur if the demon were not appeased before construction tool place on any plot of land. Only when it was content would Purusha, and the gods who imprison him, bless a building and its occupants.

THE COSMIC SQUARE

This is a poetic interpretation of the energies in the home, or indeed in any building needing to be balanced before good fortune, health and happiness can become resident in that place.

THE BODY OF PURUSHA

The Vedic diagram can be used to illustrate how the various parts of Purusha's body are represented by little squares. This form of the Vedic diagram is called the *Vastu Purusha Mandala*. According to the ancient principle of 'as above, so below' the home becomes a symbolic representation of the body, not just of Purusha, but also of the occupants of that space. Therefore each area of the home must be fully energised for maximum health benefits to its occupants.

Both the pantheon of Hindu gods and the home-demon must be appeased if good fortune is to follow.

The Vastu Purusha Mandala.

FINGERS	ELBOW	HAND	ARM	SHOULDER	NECK	EAR	EYE	**HEAD**
WRIST	ROOT OF FINGERS						MOUTH	EYE
SIDE		FINGER TIPS		**BREAST**		CHEST		EAR
SIDE								NECK
THIGH		**NAVEL**		**HEART**		**BREAST**		SHOULDER
KNEE								ARM
SHANK		GENITALS		HIPS		FINGER TIPS		HAND
BUTTOCK	GENITALS						ROOT OF FINGERS	ELBOW
FEET	BUTTOCK	THIGH	KNEE	THIGH	SIDE	SIDE	WRIST	FORE ARM

The most vital squares in the diagram are those that correspond to the heart (the precise centre of the home), the head (the extreme northwest corner), the breasts (to the north and east of the sacred centre) and the navel (to the west of the sacred centre). If these areas are harmonised correctly, an environmentally sound and spiritually tranquil interior space will be created for the benefit of all who reside or spend their time there.

THE THREE UNIVERSAL FORCES

ACCORDING TO VASTU tradition there are three distinct forces working through nature, and which are intrinsic to all the creations of the universe. These three forces are called *trigunas* collectively and *gunas* when referred to individually. The first is *sattva*, or that which holds things together. The second is *tamas*, the principle of inertia that leads to dissolution and atrophy. Finally there is *rajas*, the complex interaction between these two absolutes.

As well as representing forces that flow throughout the universe, the *trigunas* also stand for human personality types:

SATTVA

This is considered the highest and most spiritual of the three forces – the power of attraction. It also stands for growth and evolution, progress and dynamism. In human terms this force is expressed by an intelligent, creative and artistic personality type, that is pure of soul and capable of great compassion and kindness.

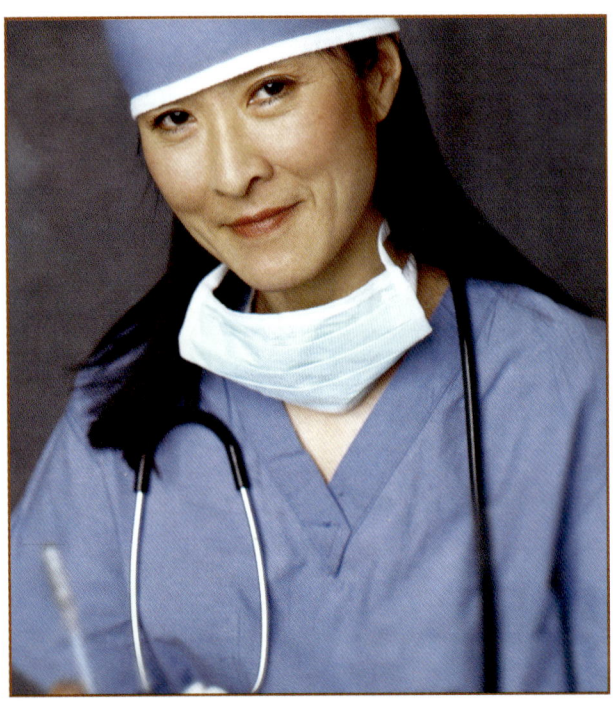
Sattva type people are capable of great compassion.

Sattva stands for growth, gradual progress and evolution.

THE THREE UNIVERSAL FORCES

TAMAS

In contrast to *sattva*, *tamas* is the principle of repulsion. This is the force that pulls things apart, prevents growth and leads to dissolution and decay. In human personality types *tamas* reveals delusion – a static personality with dull reactions and negative views. This is someone who tends to be harmful to others.

Tamas is the principle of barrenness and decay.

Tamas type people are often harmful to others.

RAJAS

Rajas is midway between the positive *sattva* and the negative *tamas*. It is a restless force, and one that varies from one extreme to the other. The principles of this *gunas* are activity and motion. People of this type tend to be ambitious and capable of hard work. They may also have strong egos and be prone to changing their minds.

A Rajas personality is restless and always "on the go".

One of the most important aims of Vastu is to harmonise the three forces in order to create healthful living conditions and maintain a positive mind and soul. There is an emphasis, therefore, on increasing the *sattva* force in one's surroundings while reducing both the negativity of *tamas* and the restless yearning of *rajas*.

AN INTRODUCTION TO VASTU

Rajas is the universal principle of motion.

THE TRIMURTI

The three *trigunas* are a vital feature of both historical and modern Hinduism and are intimately connected to the belief in the *trimurti*, the three transcendent gods who govern the cosmos. These are Brahma the creator, Vishnu the preserver and Shiva the destroyer. Vishnu, in his role as maintainer of the universe, is identified with *sattva*, while the terrible Shiva 'destroyer of worlds' is identified with the negative force of *tamas*. The restless urge to create of *rajas* remains the role for Brahma.

Sattva is particularly associated with the northeast quadrant of any dwelling so this area is of great interest. Creating harmony in this portion of the home will go a long way to receiving the benefits of *sattva* and gaining the ability live in serenity and peace.

SATVA ASSOCIATION NORTH EAST CORNER

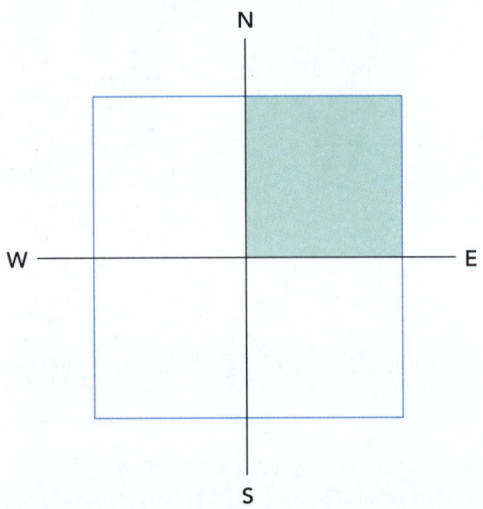

The mighty Shiva the Destroyer is the Hindu deity associated with the Tamas principle.

THE THREE UNIVERSAL FORCES

Brahma the Creator expresses the restless urge of Rajas to originate the new.

The Preserver, Vishnu keeps the universe in a state of stability and so is associated with the compassion and serenity of Sattva.

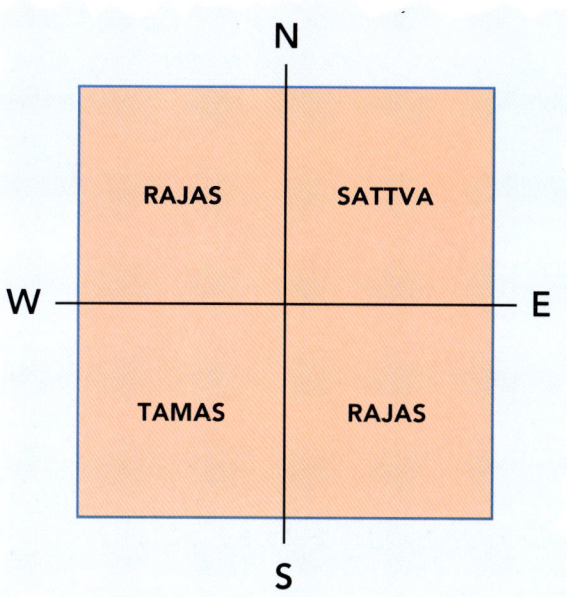

The Square of the Trigunas.

one of the *trigunas*. This square can be further divided into sections by lines from the intermediate points, creating areas that become a mixture of two *gunas*. The relative strengths of each *gunas* is represented on the following diagram as a percentage.

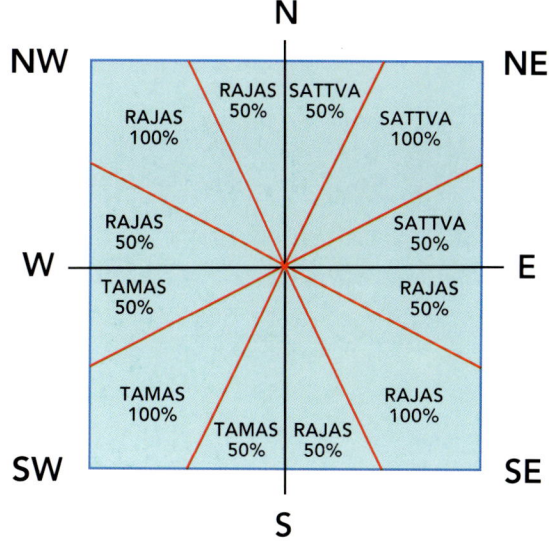

Eightfold division of the Trgunas Square.

THE SQUARE OF THE TRIGUNAS

The *trigunas* square is one of the simpler geometric forms to be found in Vastu. It is a simple quartering based on the cardinal directional points. Each of the four quadrants thus created possesses the nature of

17

AN INTRODUCTION TO VASTU

It can be seen from the diagram that those portions of the square that are influenced by *sattva* are positive in nature while those afflicted by *tamas* are negative. The north and east are dominated by a mixture of *sattva* and *rajas*, the *sattva* portion being stronger and more beneficial. Equally the south and west are areas of *tamas* and *rajas*, where the active *rajas* is more powerful.

The 100 percent influence of *sattva* in the northeastern quadrant makes this the most positive area of any living space. This is a place where clarity and a sense of spaciousness should be encouraged, and so heavy furniture should be avoided.

Large, heavy items of furniture should be reserved for the Southwest, the area of Tamas.

PRANA THE BREATH OF LIFE

In the scientific history of the Western world it was Albert Einstein who first realised that matter and energy were interchangeable. The ancient sages who formulated the theories of Vastu could have enlightened him on this point, however, because they were in no doubt that this was indeed the case.

In Vastu thinking, our bodies, all our possessions, our homes and the planet itself are merely a gross, dense form of a universal principle called *prana* or pure energy. In China this principle is called *chi* and it is the ebb and flow of this substance that forms the basis of Vastu's Oriental descendant *feng shui*. Similarly, in the beliefs of India, *chi* or *prana* is the source of all life.

A spacious, calm atmosphere should be sought in the Northeast, the direction of maximum Sattva.

The south-west on the other hand is 100 percent *tamas*, and therefore an area of dissolution, illusion and misery. Large items such as heavy furniture are perfect for this area because they provide a block to the ill fortune this may bring.

The universe and everything in it is made up of, and surrounded by, prana the cosmic breath of life.

THE THREE UNIVERSAL FORCES

Prana is created by light, life and movement.

Prana flows all around us, even within us, and is created by light, life and movement. It is the principle that animates the universe and everything within it. *Prana* flows like a gentle breeze or meandering stream while energising and enriching all living things. In Vastu belief, *prana* originates from the gateway of the gods, the northeasterly direction of the Vedic diagram. In symbolic terms, therefore, it has its beginnings in the water element (see page 23), the womb of life. For this is the reason no obstructions should be placed in the northeast because they would impede the progress of healthful *prana*. Similarly, because *prana* tends to hug the walls of a room, any furniture should be placed at least 10cm (4in) away from the wall in any room.

Prana spreads from the northeast in a clockwise direction around the sacred centre, enlivening each of the eastern and southern points of the compass in turn until it pools in the southwest. Here it may become very slow moving or even stagnant and has the potential to become harmful. For this reason, the Vastu practitioners view the southwest with suspicion. Obstructions such as bookcases and heavy items of furniture are often placed in this direction to mitigate the damage that stagnant *prana* may cause. Assuming that the *prana* of the southwest does not become totally stagnant, it will eventually progress slowly to the west and north, returning to the gateway of the gods once more before continuing its ceaseless journey towards the east and south.

For prana to flow correctly furniture should be at least 4 inches (10cm) from the nearest wall.

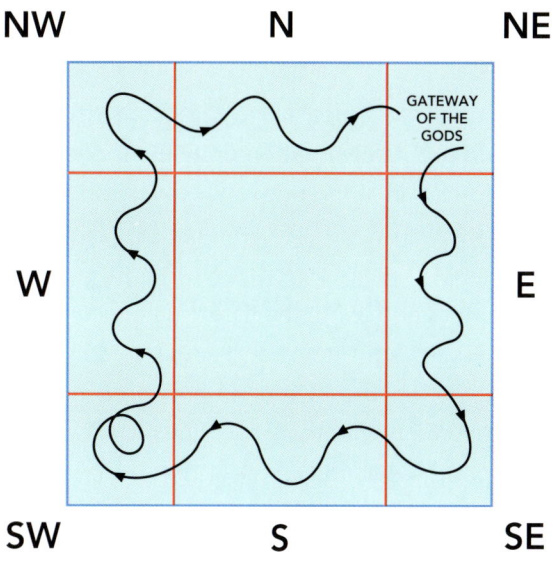

The flow of Prana from the Northeastern "Gateway of the Gods" is vital to the health and happiness of any home.

19

THE FIVE ELEMENTS

IN VEDIC TRADITION there are five forces, the *Maha Bhutas*. Each is made up of *prana*, and they are known collectively as the "five elements". The Chinese tradition of *feng shui* also recognises five forces but there are significant differences between those and the Indian originals.

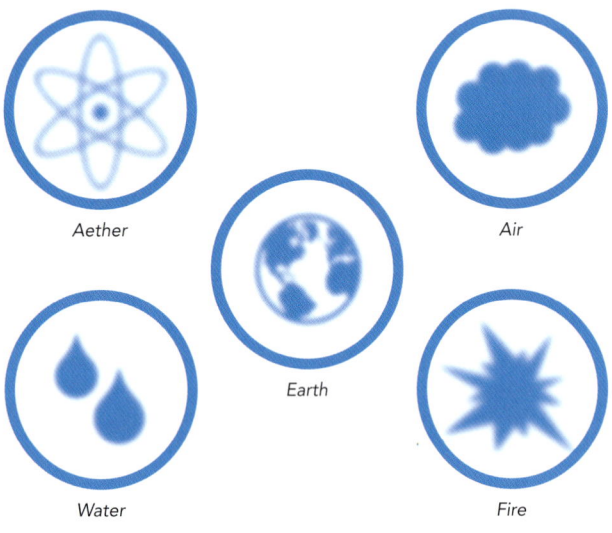

Each element has at least one direction associated with it, and has its own patron deity, symbolic shape and colours in addition its own individual characteristics. In Vastu the elements are "aether" or space, "air", "fire", "water" and "earth". These forces correspond with the five human senses of hearing, touch, sight, taste and smell. According to Vedic theory, if the five elements are properly balanced in the home, the living space will be full of positive energy and the physical body will have an increased chance of excellent health.

AETHER

The element of Aether is associated with vibrations and the sense of hearing.

The highest and most spiritual of the elements is aether. In ancient symbolism this element represents space itself and forms the background for the four remaining elements, air, fire, water and earth. It is said that vibrations flow through aether and this element therefore corresponds to the human faculty of hearing. For aether to function at its best within the home, the living space should maintain a sense of calm with pleasing sounds and a soothing atmosphere. A chaotic home is not conducive to spirituality or a clear mind, and harsh, discordant noises or a cluttered environment will tend to banish aether from its surroundings. Such a negative environment will have a very bad effect on both physical and mental health.

THE FIVE ELEMENTS

Aether is at its strongest in the most spiritual part of the home or individual room – the northeastern segment or the gateway of the gods. It is because aether functions well in calm, clean areas that the northeast in particular should be kept clear of clutter, heavy furniture and fussy decoration, allowing *prana* to enter freely. Thus the northeast is the best place for quiet thought, meditation and study.

Aether is at its strongest in the Northeastern sector. This is an ideal spot for a comfortable zone of tranquillity.

The northeast is also symbolically connected to the regent Soma the moon-god (see page 44) – a personification of the very elixir of life. Thus aether becomes associated with this regent and his mysterious regenerative potion.

The shape associated with this element is the diamond or lozenge, with important symbolic features summarised below:

Aether or Space

Direction	Northeast
Regent	Soma the moon-god
Sense	Hearing
Symbol	Diamond
Nature	Light, the Spirit, Vibration, Harmony, Divinity

AIR

The ever-restless element of air is often referred to as the "breath of Purusha" in the ancient Vedas. For Vastu beginners there may be some confusion between the concepts of aether and air, and yet they are quite different. As aether is spiritual in nature, air is intellectual. Air is associated with Vayu the wind-god – the eternally curious messenger – and to the northwesterly direction (the northwest is also linked to the water element).

The element of air is thought of as "the breath of Purusha" and is strongest in the Northwest.

A cluttered environment will disrupt the calm serenity of Aether.

21

AN INTRODUCTION TO VASTU

Both Air and Fire have Rajas energy and are considered masculine, restless and forceful.

The symbolic shape of the air element is a crescent similar to the new moon. Its most important symbolic features are summarised below:

Air	
Direction	Northwest
Regent	Vayu the wind-god
Sense	Touch
Symbol	Crescent
Nature	Transparency, Cold, Dry, Restless, Intellectual

Vayu and the air element are considered to be allies of Agni, the fire-god, who resides in the opposite direction, the southeast. Both northwest and southeast are believed to be blessed with abundant *rajas* energy making both of them forceful, restless and masculine.

In terms of the human senses, air is represented by touch. In order to ensure that this element is present in the home there should be plenty of pleasing textures. A free flow of fresh air itself is an important feature too, and attention paid to the northwest is said to ensure success in business ventures.

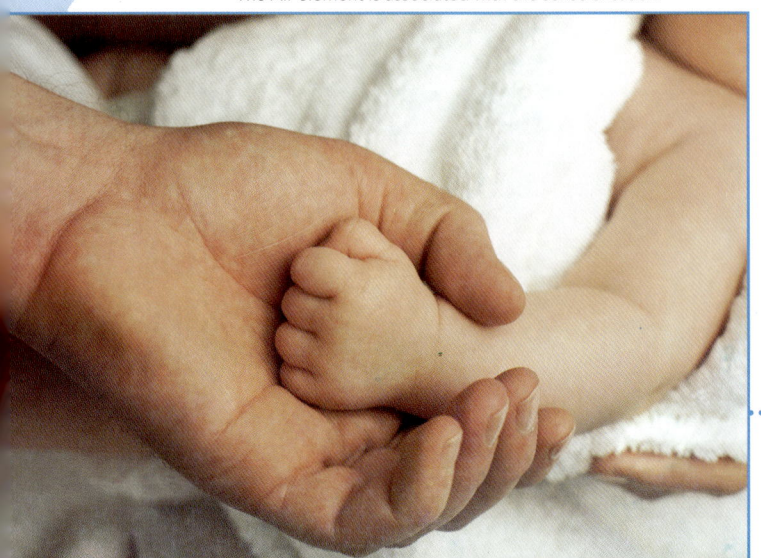

The Air element is associated with the sense of touch.

FIRE

Fire has a special significance in the beliefs of Hinduism. It is the most sacred of physical forces and the bodies of the Hindu dead are consigned to the purifying flame. The ancient sages saw fire as a mysterious, almost magical force, capable of transforming a substance into a more refined form through its heat.

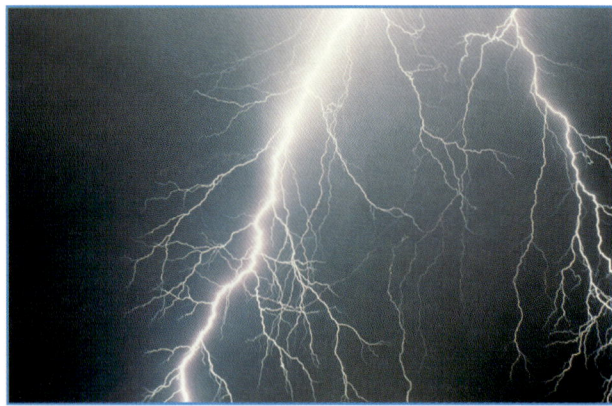

The Fire element is often found in the form of electricity.

So important is this element that, from the earliest times, it was deified as the impetuous Agni – a divine being and the regent of the southeast in the traditions of Vastu. The hot energies of Agni in the southeast

THE FIVE ELEMENTS

provide the ideal location for a kitchen because fire can also symbolise the process of digestion.

The direction of Fire, the Southeast is the best location for a kitchen.

In terms of the human senses the fire element corresponds to the most important of the senses, that of sight. In the home this element is represented by heating, lighting and electrical equipment. Absence of the element will lead to coldness in terms of both physical temperature and emotional response within a family.

Absence of Fire will lead to a coldness in temperament.

The symbolic shape associated with fire is the triangle. (Any building that is located on a triangular plot is in danger of fire.) Its most important symbolic features are summarised below:

The Fire element is associated with the sense of sight.

Fire

Direction	Southeast
Regent	Agni the fire-god
Sense	Sight
Symbol	Triangle △
Nature	Hot, Dry, Luminous, Clear, Light, Piercing

WATER

In Vastu the watery element has much in common with air. So much so, that they share the northwestern direction and the same regent, Vayu. It is a point of

The Water element is associated with the sense of taste.

interest that the Chinese system of *feng shui* literally means 'wind and water' and the northwestern segment of any room, or indeed the home in general, has a sense of ebb and flow and the movement of these two restless elements.

Water is considered to be a feminine element, signifying transitory emotions, surface feelings and business dealings. In the days when rivers were great highways of trade the watery element came to represent prosperity and the journeys one made to make a profit. Thus water, like air, is associated with movement.

The shape associated with water is the circle. (In Vastu tradition circular dwellings are not recommended unless you wish to move on in a hurry. It is interesting to note that, historically, nomadic peoples have lived in temporary homes that are circular in plan. Native Americans have their tepees, the Inuit of the Arctic have their igloos, while the Mongolian peoples of the Steppes of Asia have their dome-like yurts.)

In the human sense, water is associated with taste. In the home water is represented not just by the systems of plumbing and drainage but also with all reflective surfaces such as windows and mirrors. For this reason, the northwest is thought to be a good location for a bathroom. A guest bedroom may also be located here because its occupant will stay in your home only briefly.

The bathroom should ideally be located in the north-west.

Water	
Direction	Northwest
Regent	Vayu, the wind-god
Sense	Taste
Symbol	Circle 
Nature	Liquid, Cold, Soft, Exciting, Moving

EARTH

The final element, earth, is the most solid of all as well as being as far away as possible from the aetheric spirituality. It is therefore appropriate that earth is located in the southwest, in the opposite corner as it were, from the gateway of the gods in the northeast. Just as lightness is symbolically connected to aether, so heaviness is linked to earth. This is one of the reasons for locating the heaviest items of furniture in the south-western quadrant. The other is that the southwest comes under the rule of the regent Nirriti, a fearsome goddess who commands nightmares. Heavy objects in her sector will help banish problems by "earthing" them.

THE FIVE ELEMENTS

The Earth element is associated with the sense of smell.

The benefits of the Earth element will be harmed by the bad odours of a polluted environment.

The sense of smell is symbolically connected to the earth element so there should be plenty of pleasant fragrances in the home. A house close to sources of pollution such as factory chimneys will not enjoy the benefits of the earth element.

The positive influence of earth can also be invoked through the use of natural materials in the home – the more natural the better. Healthy indoor plants, flowers, attractive arrangements of pebbles or twigs will encourage practicality, common sense and security within the family.

Earth's symbolic shape is the square and is considered the foundation stone of the universe in Vastu terms. The square is thought to be the most fortunate shape for a permanent dwelling, allowing the balance of the other elements to function freely.

Earth	
Direction	Southwest
Regent	Nirriti
Sense	Smell
Symbol	Square □
Nature	Heavy, Rough, Dense, Hard, Inert

Attractive arrangements of pebbles or earthenware objects enhance to influence of the Earth element.

THE DOMESTIC ZODIAC

FROM THE EARLIEST TIMES, the art of Vastu Shastra has been related to the equally ancient art of astrology. The study of the stars and planets has been practised in India since before recorded history. In the Western world the zodiac of the twelve signs is usually shown as a circle. However, in India, the same information is expressed using a square. The twelve signs from Aries to Pisces are shown in a form that may be unfamiliar to us but, essentially, it is the same as the modern Western counterpart.

Since the square is the sacred shape in Vastu it is easy to see how the Vedic zodiac can be applied to the home, office, garden or any other area that is square or rectangular in shape. Aries the ram or to use Vedic terminology, Mesha, occupies the square in the eastern quarter and, moving clockwise, is followed by Taurus or Vrishna, then by Gemini or Mithuna and so on, until the square is completed by Pisces or Meena in the Northeast.

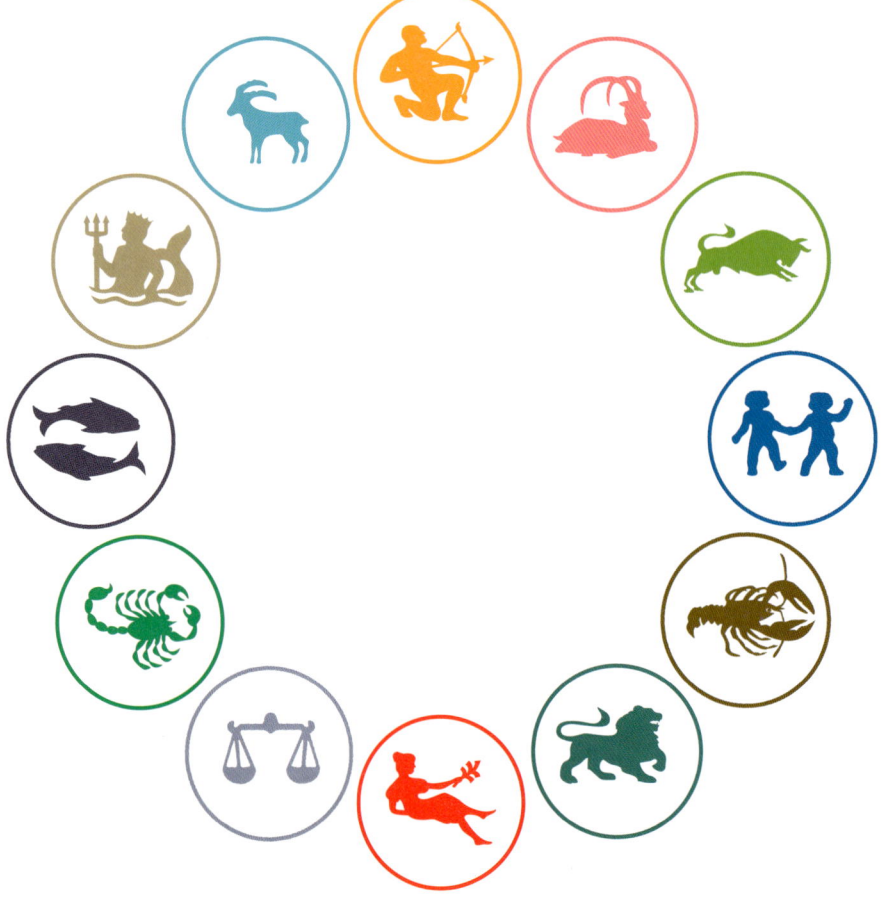

THE DOMESTIC ZODIAC

It is a fact that more people know which zodiac sign they were 'born under' than know their own blood group, so it should not be difficult to ascertain which area of one's home has particular affinity to an individual.

There is one minor difficulty in doing this, however, as the signs as shown on the Vedic diagram are not in the same place as they are on the Western chart. A complex phenomenon known as the precession of the equinoxes means that the stars are no longer in the same position as they were when the constellations were named. This has little relevance in the Western world. However, in India, it means that the constellations of the zodiac have moved one whole sign. So if in the West one considers oneself to be an Aries, born between March 20th and April 22nd then, in India, you would be counted as being born a Pisces.

Likewise a Virgo, born between August 24th and September 23rd, would be considered a Leo in the Vedic system.

At this point it is important to add that this apparent sign shift has no relevance to character reading. An Aries who now discovers that he or she is apparently a Pisces is still an Aries in Western terms. Indian astrology takes very little notice of personality traits and is more concerned with the state of one's karma and the fortune (or misfortune) that one can expect. The easiest way to deal with this apparent paradox when practising Vastu is to find your own sign in the areas of your home and then move back one in a counter-clockwise direction. In short, choose the sign before your own to find the correct area for you. Here is a little chart to help you:

THE VEDIC ZODIAC

N

SAGITTARIUS (DHANU)	CAPRICORN (MAKARA)	AQUARIUS (KUMBHA)	PISCES (MEENA)
SCORPIO (VRISHCHIKA)	SACRED CENTRE		ARIES (MESHA)
LIBRA (TULA)			TAURUS (VRISHNA)
VIRGO (KANYA)	LEO (SIMHA)	CANCER (KARKA)	GEMINI (MITHUNA)

W   E

S

WESTERN ZODIAC SIGN	DATES	VASTU ZODIAC SHIFT
Aries the Ram	21st Mar – 20th Apr	Pisces (Meena)
Taurus the Bull	21st Apr – 21st May	Aries (Mesha)
Gemini the Twins	22nd May – 21st Jun	Taurus (Vrishna)
Cancer the Crab	22nd Jun – 23rd Jul	Gemini (Mithuna)
Leo the Lion	24th Jul – 23rd Aug	Cancer (Karka)
Virgo the Virgin	24th Aug – 23rd Sep	Leo (Simha)
Libra the Scales	24th Sep – 23rd Oct	Virgo (Kanya)
Scorpio the Scorpion	24th Oct – 22nd Nov	Libra (Tula)
Sagittarius the Archer	23rd Nov – 21st Dec	Scorpio (Vrishchika)
Capricorn the Goat	22nd Dec – 20th Jan	Sagittarius (Dhanu)
Aquarius the Water Bearer	21st Jan – 19th Feb	Capricorn (Makara)
Pisces the Fish	20th Feb – 20th Mar	Aquarius (Kumbha)

PLANETARY PLACEMENTS

THE ANCIENT ART of astrology has had a profound influence on Indian culture as a whole and on Vastu in particular. We have already seen how the signs of the zodiac relate to various directions and areas within the home. Now this can be taken to another level by including the influences of the seven traditional planets.

Historically, seven planets or 'wanderers' were known to the ancient world. The sun and moon are included here as planets even though the sun is our parent star while the moon is a satellite of the earth. The seven traditional planets are the sun or Surya, the moon or Chandra, Mercury or Budha, Venus or Shukra, Mars or Kuja, Jupiter or Guru and finally, Saturn or Shani. The

so-called modern planets Uranus, Neptune, Pluto and Chiron are not visible to the naked eye and were therefore unknown to the sages of ancient India.

In astrology, each of the heavenly bodies is considered to have a distinct personality, specific functions and associations. So, in the minds of astrologers and practitioners of Vastu alike, there is a relationship between the characteristics of the planets and activities within the home.

As usual in Vastu the planets are allocated a direction of the compass. However, unlike the directions given to the zodiac signs (see page 28) and to the regents (see page 38), specific planetary alignments within the home are not so vital. Far more important is the correlation of any given planet to human activity within an allocated space and how its power can be helped or hindered through the choice of colour and associated symbols in each area of the home.

SURYA THE SUN

The most powerful influence in the horoscope is undoubtedly that of the sun. While the sun is a benign influence in Western astrology this is not necessarily the case from an Indian point of view. For example, the sun is not a divinity in Hinduism but a demon – the withering, parching heat from our parent star is not something to be welcomed. Hence Western associations of joy and music are

NW	N	NE
MOON (CHANDRA) BATHROOM GUEST BEDROOM	MOON (GURU) OFFICE/STUDY LIBRARY VALUABLES	MOON (SURYA) ZONE OF TRANQUILITY
MOON (BUDHA) LOUNGE DINING ROOM	SACRED CENTRE	MOON (SHUKRA) BEDROOM CHILD'S ROOM
MOON (SHANI) CUPBOARDS WARDROBE CELLAR	MOON (SHUKRA) BEDROOM	MOON (KUJA) KITCHEN ELECTRICAL EQUIPMENT
SW	S	SE

THE PLANETS AND THE HOME AND IDEAL LOCATIONS

PLANETARY PLACEMENTS

missing from the Indian system. Instead there is an emphasis on sheltering from the fiery blast of the sun's strong rays. This has led to Surya being associated with far more passive pursuits than would be the case in the West.

The sun is associated with meditation in Vastu symbolism. It represents the heart and, in more symbolically, the true inner self or the soul, known as *atman*. This is the one imperishable part of us, the immortal portion which, in the beliefs of both Hinduism and Buddhism, moves on from life to life abandoning each mortal body in turn to find a new existence and experience. The solar portion of the home is, therefore, the most spiritual area.

Traditionally this is the northeastern quarter – that which is least likely to be affected by the midday heat. In practical terms, any area that has an aura of calm and quiet is governed by Surya. A décor of light blue is said to enhance inward contemplation and a quest for inner perfection.

In southern India the harsh heat of the sun is not considered benign as it is in the west.

The sun's influence encourages inward contemplation in the cool of the shade.

CHANDRA THE MOON

The idea of motherhood is inextricably linked to the symbolism of the moon in both Western and Eastern astrology. Equally, the moon is associated with the instinctive self and the subconscious mind. To the sages of the ancient world the monthly cycle of the moon as it progressed from new to full to new again was reminiscent of a process of eternal renewal. The new moon was indicative of youth and virginity, the full moon represented pregnancy and the waning moon, the gestation period. The following new moon was therefore symbolic of birth.

The moon is connected to the water element and, just as our satellite rules the ocean tides, its waxing and waning was considered to

AN INTRODUCTION TO VASTU

The influence of the new moon is symbolic of birth and maternal virtues.

The bathroom is a place of renewal and cleansing governed by the moon.

be the perfect expression of the forces of nature both outside us in the universe and within the depths of our own beings. In Vastu terms, the concepts of refreshment and renewal are associated with the lunar part of the home. The bathroom is ruled by both the moon and by the watery element. Ideally, it should be situated in the northeast of a home because this is the direction most associated with the moon's influence. In practice, however, it can be placed anywhere as long as certain lunar guidelines are followed. The most fortunate colours for this area are light greens and blues, and white. Lighting should be soft and relaxing to allow for spiritual as well as physical cleansing.

BUDHA OR MERCURY

Swift Mercury is the smallest and fastest of the planets. As in the Western world, Mercury is associated with communication in Eastern tradition and is known as Budha. The word Budha is derived from the Sanskrit *buddhi* meaning analysis or intellectual reasoning. It is also interesting to note that the founder of the Buddhist religion was a messenger of the universe, preaching a doctrine of infinite compassion. Another correlation between East and West is the planet's symbolic role as the messenger of the gods.

Budha was the messenger of the universe to mankind. He is identified with the planet Mercury.

32

PLANETARY PLACEMENTS

Pleasant and informative conversations are associated with Mercury.

Mercury governs the dining room where relaxed family discussions can take place.

SHUKRA OR VENUS

In both Western and Eastern astrology, Venus is considered to be extremely sensual, feminine in nature, and to have the ability to promote pleasure in human beings. Concepts associated with the planet named after the goddess of love include softness,

One important aspect of the planet's influence is that of pleasant and informative conversation. This implies a relaxed atmosphere, freedom of expression and sociability. The area most associated with Mercury, therefore, is the living room or dining area – rooms where lively and amusing discussion can take place. Mercury's influence of the living and relaxing area of the home is a vital one. Here the family can discuss the events of the day, the aspirations of life and air and diffuse any worries. To help this process along, the inclusion of light blue in this space will ease communication and put people in a more relaxed frame of mind.

Venus is associated with softness, comfort and luxury.

33

AN INTRODUCTION TO VASTU

When considering a Venus area of the home never forget that sensuality and luxury are a must.

luxury and beauty. It is therefore logical that the area of the home allocated to this divine temptress should be the bedroom. In this sense the bedroom is not to be considered just a place for sleeping as it is in *feng shui*. In Vastu making love is the primary function of this space. Indeed, the Indian word *shukra* literally means semen and, further, Venus is considered to provide the ability to conceive. Vastu tradition holds that the bedroom must be luxurious and sensual.

The planet of love governs the bedroom which should be a place of romance.

Venus is allocated two directions, the east and the south, although it is not the direction but the atmosphere that is the most important factor here. The bedroom should be a separate space, far removed from the duties and trials of daily life. This should be a place to relax, to enjoy life and to sink into beautiful repose and thereby enter a world of heavenly dreams. To enhance this playful atmosphere it is important that the bedroom be Venusian in nature. The colours pink, light blue and chrome yellow should be included in here, as should soft furnishings, large cushions and anything that leads the mind to thoughts of love. Erotic artwork and a copy of the *Karma Sutra* are optional.

There should be plenty of cushions and soft furnishings in a Venus area.

KUJA OR MARS

In Western astrology the red planet Mars is considered to be the indicator of masculine force. It is usually associates with personal drive and dynamism. However, in India, a more old-fashioned view prevails and Mars is most often thought of as the creator of violence, upheaval and wrath. Even though modern astronomy does not concur, the traditional nature of the red planet is hot and fiery. Symbolically, it is related to iron and sharp bladed weapons. In Vastu terms then, the natural place for this planet within the home is the kitchen.

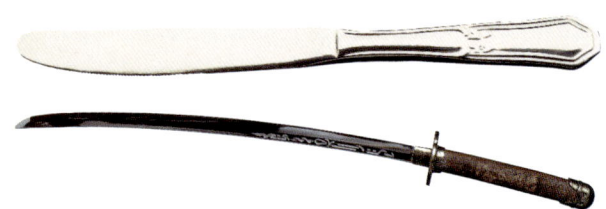

Mars or Kuja is associated with blades and sharp objects.

Vedic tradition allocates the kitchen to the fire element because this is the place that cooking is done. It is also in the kitchen that sharp blades can be found in the shape of carving knives and other cutting implements. The natural direction for this potentially

34

PLANETARY PLACEMENTS

harmful planet is the southeast, ruled by the fiery regent Agni (see page 39). However, as with the other planets, it is the use of an area rather than its compass direction that is important here. Great care must be taken in accommodating wrathful Mars in the kitchen area, as a failure to do so may result in quarrels, domestic disharmony and even family break-up. The simplest way of achieving this is by including the colour red in the décor of the cooking area.

GURU OR JUPITER

In Vastu the enormous planet Jupiter is known as Guru or 'the teacher'. In the Western world the influence of this giant planet is related to belief systems, to religion, philosophy and any sort of mental or spiritual journey. Likewise, in India, Guru is considered to be the instructor of the assembly of the gods. Concepts related to the influence of this planet include those of illumination or the sudden realisation of truth. This is the greatest wealth that one can possess. Jupiter also governs the more material aspect of riches, however, and is an indication of worldly treasures. In terms of human space, the natural place for Jupiter is a library, study or home office.

A Guru or Jupiter area is an ideal location for a home office.

Such places are also considered to be the best areas in which to keep treasured or valuable items and Jupiter therefore signifies security of both the mind and the material world.

Guru is associated with the knowledge enshrined in books.

The natural direction for this planet is the north but, as with the other planets, the specific use of the space is the important factor for planetary influence. Therefore, any study area or a place where repositories of knowledge, such as books, are kept is ruled by wise Jupiter. A good colour scheme for any such area is yellow, an enhancer of mental activity.

AN INTRODUCTION TO VASTU

Treasured items are best kept in an area governed by Jupiter.

Too much dark furniture will be "saturnine" and provide a depressive influence to the home.

SHANI OR SATURN

Saturn is the furthest planet from the earth that is visible to the naked eye. To the ancient sages who formulated the arts of astrology, therefore, this planet came to represent boundaries because beyond its orbit lay the vast depths of space. It is ironic that modern telescopes have since revealed Saturn to be orbited by a vast ring of debris because, symbolically, this planet encompasses the idea of being enclosed. Saturn is considered to be the ponderous, steady arbiter of time as well as being associated with rules and regulations, confinement, old age, duty and self-denial. In Vedic lore Saturn or Shani is associated with the harmful vibrations of the southwest and, in practice, it governs all dark places within the home. Cellars, basements, cupboards and dingy corners all fall within the symbolic orbit of gloomy Saturn.

Shani or Saturn, is associated with the passage of time, with loss and old age.

PLANETARY PLACEMENTS

In keeping with Saturn's grim reputation, its associated colour is black. Therefore any item or piece of furniture within the home that is very dark in colour will share some of the symbolism of the ringed planet. It should be noted that being surrounded by too much black has the same affect as being constantly in the dark, which could not fail to be a depressing influence.

Now we have a home that not only relates to the signs of the zodiac but where the functions of each space in the home have their own symbolic resonance with the seven traditional planets.

THE SHADOW PLANETS

Hindu astrology also features two so-called 'shadow planets' named Rahu and Ketu or 'the dragon's head' and 'the dragon's tail' respectively. These are the points at which the celestial path of the moon crosses that of the sun. In the Western world these are known as the nodes of the moon and are always directly opposite each other in the zodiac.

In Hindu belief these nodes relate to the passing of the soul from life to life. Ketu is indicative of the fortunes of the last life on earth and therefore has a bearing on one's present *karma*. Rahu represents the destiny that must be played out in the present life as well as being indicative of the karmic debt or rewards one has incurred.

Since these shadow planets have no objective existence, they do not play a part in the home. However the inclusion of Rahu and Ketu in Hindu astrology brings the planetary count up to nine- the significant number forming the basis of the cosmic square.

Rahu and Ketu are so-called "shadow planets" connected with karma. They bring the planetary total up to nine.

THE REGENTS OF SPACE

THE *PARAMASHAYIKA* or Vedic square is made up of eighty-one smaller squares, which serve to show the influence of the eight compass directions (see page 9). Each direction has a presiding force, symbolised by a Hindu deity. These personified forces are called vasu or "regents".

INDRA – LORD OF THE THUNDERBOLT

Each individual regent has distinct attributes and qualities that have a direct bearing on human existence. The Vedic square is said to begin at the eastern quarter, and it is here that Indra, the king of

NW	N	NE
VAYA LORD OF THE WIND	**KUBERA** LORD OF WEALTH	**SOMA** LORD OF THE MOON
VARUNA LORD OF THE OCEAN, FATE AND MYSTERIES	**BRAHMA** THE CREATOR	**INDRA** LORD OF RENEWAL
NIRRITI LORD OF SLEEP, GHOSTS AND DEMONS	**YAMA** LORD OF JUSTICE, KARMA AND DEATH	**AGNI** LORD OF FIRE
SW	S	SE

(W on middle-left, E on middle-right)

THE REGENTS OF SPACE

THE REGENTS OF SPACE

Indra, the Regent of the East is lord of the thunderbolt.

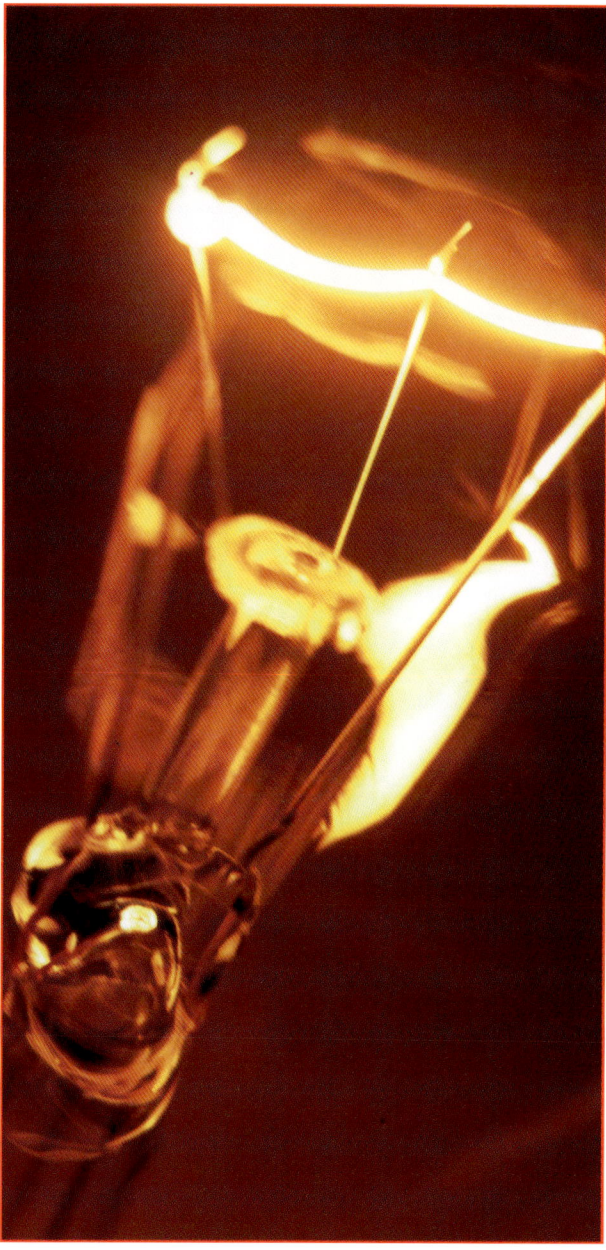

In a modern Home Agni, lord of fire is also associated with electricity.

the Vedic gods, is located. Indra is portrayed as being a beautiful, regal king with golden skin and riding an elephant – the symbol of his majesty. As with the more familiar Jupiter or Zeus of classical mythology, Indra is considered to be the lord of the thunderbolt. He is therefore associated with electricity and anything that provides power and motivating force.

AGNI – LORD OF FIRE

Just as the sun moves across the sky in a clockwise direction, we now move to the southeastern quarter and the area governed by the mighty Agni, the eternally youthful fire-god. This deity is usually shown as a vigorous young man, red in colour, with a garland

AN INTRODUCTION TO VASTU

of fruit around his neck. Like many other Hindu gods, Agni is blessed with more than the usual quota of heads and limbs. He has three faces and seven arms.

This fiery regent rides a ram and is credited with the power to provide illumination both in the physical world and in the more spiritual realms of the soul.

This is a strongly solar region of the home, the heat of the sun providing Agni with his fire.

THE REGENTS OF SPACE

Tombs and ancestors are associated with Yama, the lord of the departed.

YAMA – GOD OF DEATH

The regent of the south is the awesome Yama, god of death, ruler of the souls of the departed and the arbiter of justice. Some strands of early Indian belief state that Yama was in fact the first man – the Vedic equivalent of the Biblical Adam. He was, therefore, the first man to die and, having done so, took possession of an empty kingdom. Since it is the nature of mortals to pass on, Yama soon gained many subjects for his new kingdom. Although to a Western mind, the allocation of the death-god to the south may seem strange, it should be remembered that Yama is also the guardian of the past and the codes of ethics and values of our ancestors.

NIRRITI – LADY OF NIGHTMARES

A far more sinister figure is the regent of the southwest. This is the grim-natured goddess Nirriti. Grinning balefully, she is depicted standing upon a corpse or riding a lion. In her four arms she bears a javelin, a sword, a shield and a staff. Nirriti presides over the unquiet dead – ghosts, demons and the horrors of the imagination. As a result, her direction is considered to be the fount of many ills, poverty, unhappiness and discontent. Nirriti is said to favour those who gamble, probably because this habit causes so many of the troubles that seem to delight this malevolent goddess.

Nirriti favours gamblers because this habit causes so much misery.

VARUNA – THE SEA-GOD

Varuna, the sea-god, is the regent of the west – the direction of the setting sun. Varuna is depicted riding a sea monster that combines the features of a crocodile with those of an ox. (This creature is actually used as the equivalent to our astrological sign of Capricorn in the Vedic zodiac, where it is called Makara). The lord of the depths of the ocean is an apt symbol for the west because Varuna governs all that is mysterious and hidden from sight. It is said that this regent's power is most evident during the hours of darkness when the secrets of the unconscious mind are revealed in dreams.

THE REGENTS OF SPACE

VAYU – THE WIND-GOD

The northwest is the realm of Vayu, the wind-god, and messenger of the Vedic gods. This swift deity rides a fleet-footed deer and bears a bow and arrow. Vayu is considered to be a powerful regent with a might that can flatten mountains and uproot trees if that is his desire. Vayu is also considered to be a close friend of the fiery Agni (who occupies the diagonally opposite square). Just as the wind will fan a flame, Vayu is said to strengthen and encourage Agni and the youthful exuberance of his direction.

Varuna is the lord of the ocean symbolising the depths of the unconscious mind.

Vayu, lord of the air is associated with the tops of mountains and the restless movement of the wind in the trees.

AN INTRODUCTION TO VASTU

KUBERA – LORD OF WEALTH

The regent of the north is portrayed as an ugly dwarf by the name of Kubera, who dwells among the high peaks of the Himalayan Mountains. Kubera is thought to possess three legs and eight teeth and, despite his unprepossessing appearance, is considered to be the lord of wealth and mineral resources. Possibly to counteract his ugliness, Kubera is habitually shown smothered in gold and precious gems. By association the north is the direction of prosperity.

The ugly, dwarf-god Kubera is the guardian of wealth and precious gems.

SOMA – THE MOON-GOD

The last directional regent is Soma, the moon-god, who governs the northeast. Round-faced and pale, Soma is also thought to be a personification of a magical nectar of the same name. This nectar is equivalent to the 'elixir of eternal life' considered to be the source of the power of Indra. The word Soma was also used to describe an intoxicating liquor that was, and possibly still is, consumed at religious festivals. The northeast is therefore associated with health, wellbeing and joy.

BRAHMA – THE CREATOR

The central square of the Vedic diagram has no direction but does possess a regent. In this case it is the most important regent of all, Brahma the creator, architect of the cosmos.

It is a basic belief of practitioners of Vastu that the influence of the regents can be felt in daily life and that their power is evident in the direction over which they rule.

Soma the moon-god is said to brew the elixir of eternal life. He bestows wellbeing and joy.

THE REGENTS OF SPACE

DIRECTION	EMBODIMENT	SYMBOL	STONE	IN THE HOME
east	Indra, lord of renewal, fertility and children	thunderbolt	diamond	child's room, bathroom (not toilet)
southeast	Agni, lord of fire, potent energies, health and women's issues	fire	coral	kitchen, fireplace, electrical equipment
south	Yama, lord of death, law, justice and *karma*	club	sapphire	bedroom, bathroom, spare room, storage
southwest	Nirriti, lady of sleep, ghosts and demons who can give fame, longevity and wealth	dagger	cat's eye	bedroom, bathroom, spare room, home office and storage
west	Varuna, lord of the ocean and rain, god of fate, the mysterious, *karma* and male issues	lasso	emerald	living room, library, bedroom
northwest	Vayu, lord of the wind, governing communication, social life and business	antelope or deer	topaz	dining room, kitchen, bathroom and guest bedrooms
north	Kubera, lord of wealth and precious stones governing prosperity and career	mongoose	pearl	library, study, home office, bedroom, dressing rooms
northeast	Soma, lord of the moon and the nectar of the gods, governing spiritual knowledge	vase or urn	moonstone	shrines and areas set aside for meditation
centre	Brahma, the creator, who grants creativity and equilibrium	book	ruby	the central area of the house, be it a courtyard or a living room

APPLYING VASTU

HAVING BEEN INTRODUCED to the new concepts of fire and wind lines, domestic zodiac signs, planetary rooms, the five elements, the three universal forces and the nine regents of space, there is now the question of how to get to grips with Vastu. This does not have to be as confusing as it sounds and, by following simple guidelines and taking one step at a time, it will not take long to master this ancient art. Below is an essential guide to everything you need to do in order to apply the principles of Vastu to your home.

Using an ordinary directional compass and some graph paper, draw a rough floor plan of your home. This will be easy if you live in an apartment. If you live in a house of more than one story then at least two floor plans will be required, one for each floor.

It does not need to be 100 percent accurate, but you should measure up to make sure that you are not too far off the mark. Draw in the doors, windows and other physical features.

ADAPTING THE SQUARE

In Vastu, the square is the most sacred symbol, representing the universe, and it is this shape that is used to determine how your home is to be divided into separate areas. However, it is unlikely that your living space will be exactly this shape. If you have a rectangular home, simply elongate the Vastu square to fit your particular space. If you live in a space that is

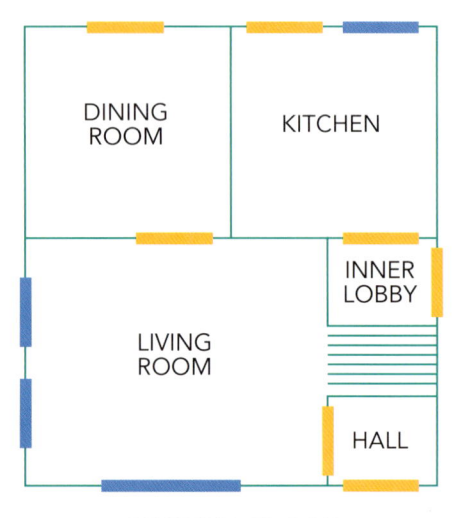

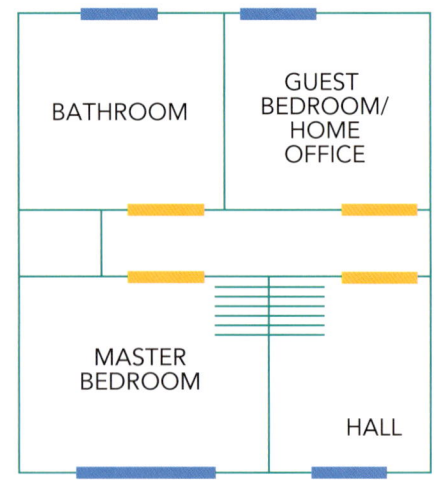

Drawing your floor plan.

APPLYING VASTU

irregular in shape, having 'wings', shaped like an 'H' or possibly 'L', then there are several options open to you. You can either 'square off' the missing section or sections, filling in the missing area with a dotted line. Or you can create two or more separate areas, each a square or rectangle.

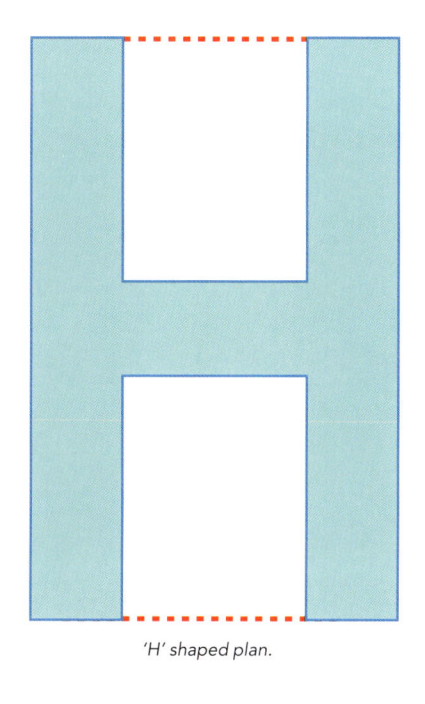

'H' shaped plan.

'L' shaped plan.

FINDING THE CENTRE

Now it is time to find the exact centre of your home. This is achieved by drawing two diagonal lines from corner to corner. The point at which they cross is the sacred centre, the area of the regent Brahma. If your home is aligned to the cardinal compass directions, north, south, east and west, these diagonal lines will also be the wind lines (see page 9). It is a good idea to use different coloured pens to prevent confusion between the walls of your dwelling and the theoretical divisions found in Vastu.

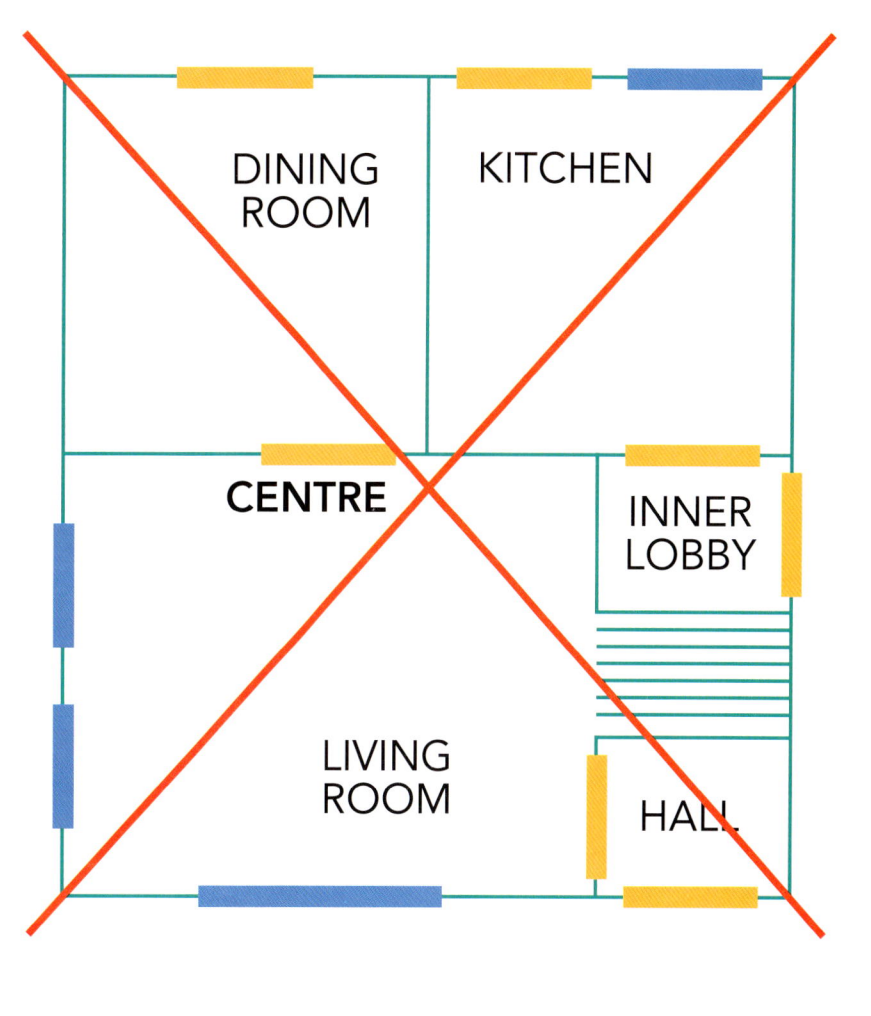

It is important to keep the centre of your home, or indeed any room clear and tranquil to gain the maximum benefits from Vastu.

AN INTRODUCTION TO VASTU

FINDING THE REGENTS

Having completed the rough scale drawing of your home you can now stand at the centre with your directional compass. Carefully mark the cardinal directions north, south, east and west on your floor plan. By doing this you will have found the fire line (north to south) and the "sunrise line" (east to west). This action has also marked the regents Kubera (north), Yama (south), Indra (east) and Varuna (west). Finding the other four regents is now easy because they occupy the spaces between the cardinal directions.

Each of the eight regents resides in a small square within the larger square that represents your home. If you have used graph paper and your floor plans are as accurate as possible, you should now be able to divide your home into nine equal squares, each corresponding to the regents of space with Brahma in the sacred centre.

You will now have a floor plan complete with the eight major directional compass points and a simple grid of nine squares. You will also have found the fire lines along the cardinal directions and the wind lines which operate diagonally.

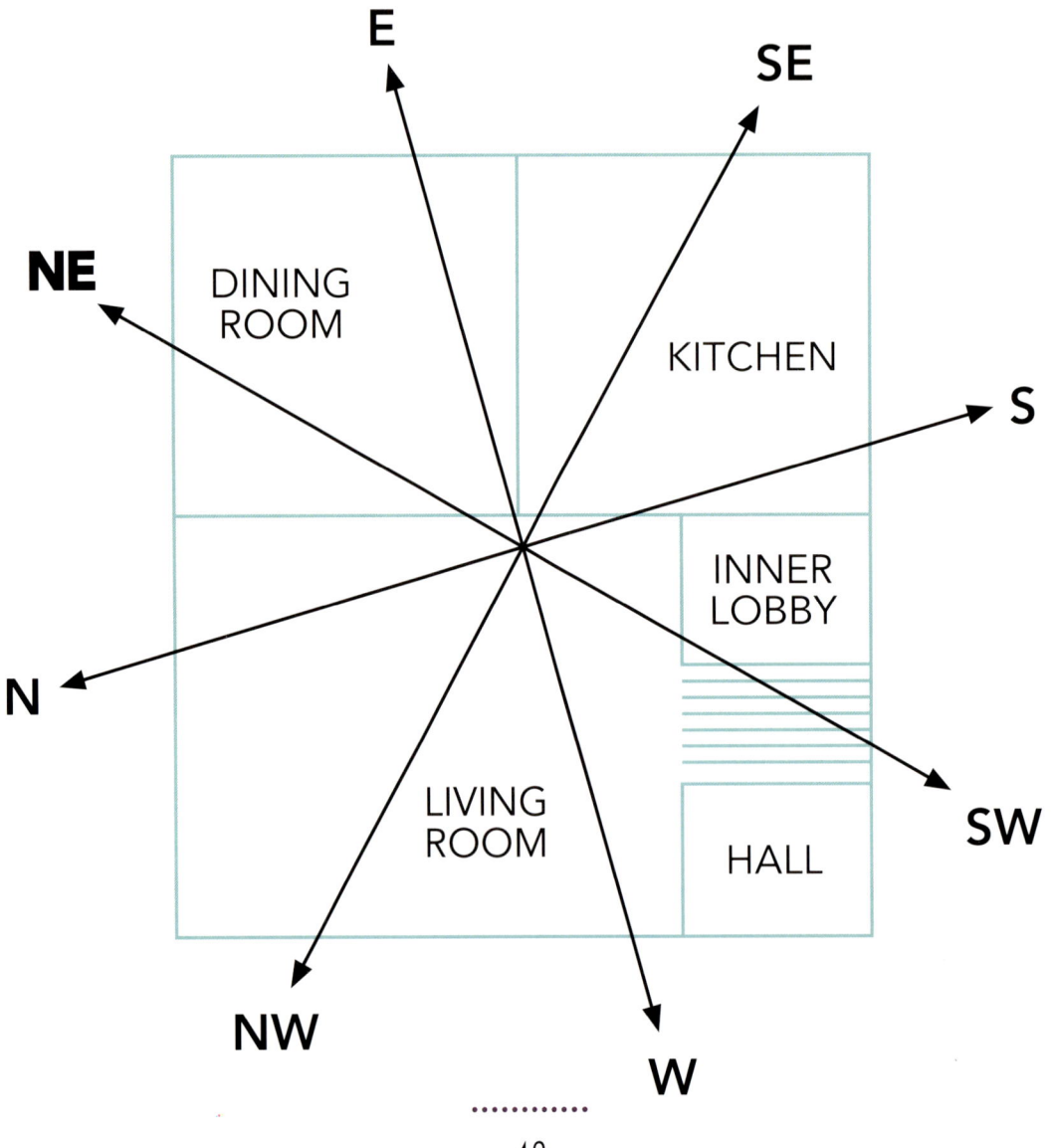

APPLYING VASTU

FINDING THE DOMESTIC ZODIAC

It is now time to find the areas that are occupied by the zodiac signs and the planets. The zodiac signs can be worked out quite simply (see page 28). Stand at the centre of your home and face east, looking in the direction of the furthest wall of your property. The area to your immediate left corresponds to the sign of Aries. The area to your right is Taurus. Gemini then follows at the right-hand corner with Pisces at the furthest left-hand corner.

If you now look to the south, the area to your left is taken by Cancer, and that to your right, by Leo. Virgo occupies the corner on the furthest right in the ill-omened southwest. Facing west, Libra is on the left of the furthest wall while Scorpio is on the right. Sagittarius occupies the furthest corner to your right in the northwest.

When facing north, Sagittarius is in the corner furthest to your left, while immediately to your left is the sign of Capricorn. The sign of Aquarius is on your immediate right. This brings us back to Pisces, which occupies the northeastern corner of your home.

Remember that there is a difference of one whole sign between Western and Vedic astrology (see page 29), so if you are a Scorpio in Western terms you will be a Libran in Vedic law. Likewise, an Aries will be counted as a Pisces and a Gemini as a Taurus and so on. Bearing this in mind, you can now find the area of the home in which you will be most comfortable.

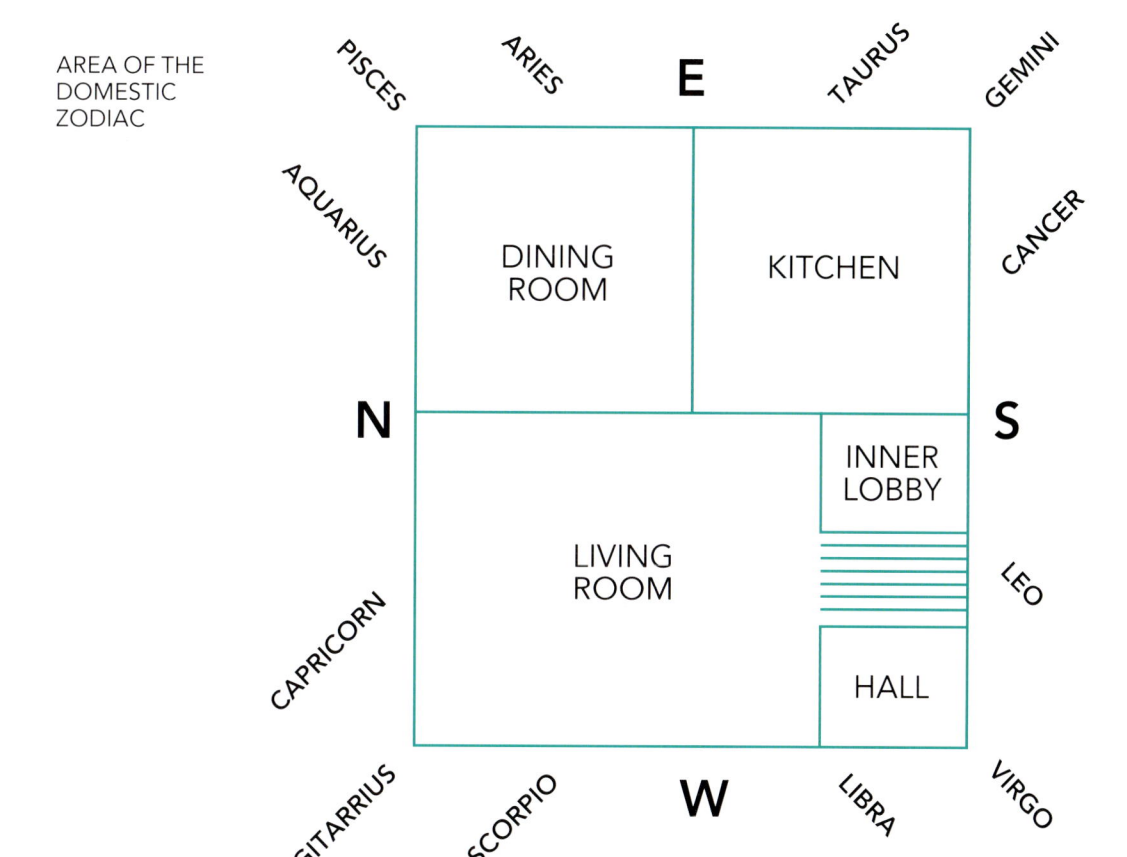

AREA OF THE DOMESTIC ZODIAC

AN INTRODUCTION TO VASTU

FINDING THE PLANETS

The influence of each planet on the home is not governed by fixed directional positions, but on the specific use a room is put to. For example, a living room will always be influenced by the communicative planet Mercury, no matter where the room is located within the home, and in spite of the fact that the ideal position for a living room is in the west. This is true for all rooms of the house.

Returning to your graph paper, use the diagram of planetary placements to locate the rooms in your home. Remember that this diagrams shows the ideal locations of these rooms and not necessarily those that apply in your own home.

Establishing the planet associated with each room of your home will provide guidelines for décor, furnishings and embellishments in order to create maximum good fortune.

Planetary placemnt.

THE ZONE OF TRANQUILLITY

Vastu tradition insists that an area in every room of the house should be set aside for meditation and quiet contemplation. This area is known as the "tranquillity zone". A calm and comfortable atmosphere can be created by placing a light chair here, by introducing some healthy plants and by using soft lighting. If space is in short supply, for example in a kitchen, a picture that inspires a spiritual moment would serve as a calming focal point. Of course, the home itself should have a main tranquillity zone, and Vastu tradition recommends that this be located in the northeastern quadrant, the very source of healthful *prana*, also referred to as the gateway of the gods.

Healthy plants, tastefully arranged are a good idea in the tranquillity zone.

APPLYING VASTU

Mood lighting can be used to great effect in the tranquil area.

The bathroom is governed by water and can cause problems if located in the fire area.

PROBLEMS AND APPEASEMENTS

Those who are new to Vastu can become confused by the inevitable problems associated with the placement of rooms in inconvenient areas of the home. It is one thing to move a sofa or heavy bookcase, it is quite another to move an entire kitchen or bathroom! Fortunately, such drastic steps are never necessary, as there are a series of remedies known as "appeasements" for the event that a bathroom – ideally governed by water – may be located in the southeast – the area governed by fire. Or for a kitchen – governed by fire – being located in the northwest, which is influenced by water and air.

Appeasements fall into two distinct categories. One remedy is to use colour and décor to re-establish harmony. The alternative is to represent the regent of a particular area by using appropriate symbolic objects or images. Since most appeasements involve both the area one is dealing with and where that area is located in the home, it is not unusual to need two appeasements in order for harmony to be re-established.

If the kitchen is in the water area an appeasement by the use of suitable colours will be an effective remedy.

AN INTRODUCTION TO VASTU

APPEASEMENT BY USE OF SYMBOLS AND COLOUR

A Problem in the East

The east is governed by the regent Indra, wielder of the thunderbolt and god of renewal. Both Aries and Taurus and the planet Venus have an influence here as well. This area is associated with intelligence, the thought process, youthfulness, growth and children, especially boys. It is a good spot, therefore, for a bedroom or child's room. It is not suitable for basement entrances, a w.c., for keeping valuables or as a meditation area. If any of these are situated here, then the symbolic solution would be to introduce an image of Indra himself or a representation of one of his attributes such as an elephant, a diamond or a thunderbolt. In terms of colour, white or green could be included in the décor as an acceptable alternative.

A white horse (associated with Varuna) is a good feature in a child's room encouraging colt-like energy during the day and good dreams at night.

Anything suggestive of a diamond will serve as an appeasement to Indra.

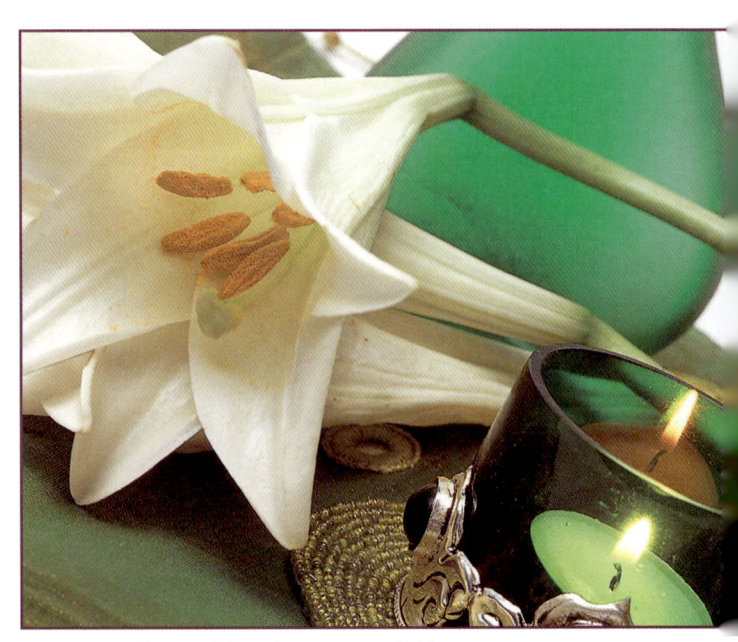

The use of the colours green and white serve as an appeasement to Indra and the East.

APPLYING VASTU

Anything reminiscent of heat and light are suitable appeasements to Agni.

A Problem in the Southeast

The southeast is governed by the fire-god Agni and the fire element. It is also associated with the planet Mars and the sign of Gemini. This is the perfect place for the kitchen and an ideal location for electrical equipment. It is not a suitable sector for a bedroom, a meditation area or a bathroom. Should any of these be located in this quadrant of the home, a symbolic solution would be to include a statuette of Agni or Mars or an image of a ram (the mount of Agni and symbol of the sign of Aries). Candles and anything triangular – the symbolic shape of the fire element – or reminiscent of heat and fire would also serve as an acceptable appeasement. In terms of décor, introduce reds, yellows and oranges.

Candles are very useful to appease Agni and the Fire element.

A Problem in the South

This is the direction of Yama, the just god of *karma* and ruler of the dead. It is the direction of the ancestors and those who have passed beyond this life. A bedroom in this sector is considered to be ideal, since it will inspire peaceful rest. A front door, a study area, and a living or dining room, however, are not recommended here. Any representation of the death-god is not a good idea anywhere in the home, even if, as in Hindu belief, he is benevolent. However, an image of a cow or bull will work here. The best possible appeasement in the south is to use photographs of beloved family members who have passed on and are now blessed subjects of Yama. The presiding planet of bedrooms is Venus, so pinks and light greens can provide an alternative appeasement.

The cow, sacred in India is associated with Yama and the South.

A bedroom in the South may be decorated in pinks, one of the colours of Venus.

A Problem in the Southwest

This is the most dangerous and problematic area, associated with the dreadful Nirriti, regent of sleep, ghosts and nightmares. The southwest is also associated with the grim planet Saturn and the element of earth. This is not a bad location for a bedroom, but care must be taken to ensure that the extreme southwestern corner of the room has something large and heavy in it in order to prevent

Using purple tones can appease Nirriti.

An image of a lion would be a suitable appeasement to Nirriti.

positive energy from escaping. This sector would suit an entrance to a basement or cellar or would make the perfect location for wardrobes, heavy bookcases and other forms of bulky furniture. This is the worst possible direction for the front door and is an unsuitable location for a kitchen. The simplest appeasement is to place one's heavy furniture in this sector, but you can also appease Nirriti and Saturn by using an image of the goddess riding her lion here (a statuette of a lion or other big cat may also be used). Other images suggesting night and darkness are also acceptable. A colour solution would be to use purple or violet in the décor.

A Problem in the West

The west is intellectual and communicative in nature. It is associated with the deeply thoughtful Varuna, god of the ocean and with the swift-witted planet Mercury. This is a social area in which animated conversations can occur and, therefore, it is not the best area for a bedroom, meditation area or kitchen. An image of Hindu Varuna or of Roman Mercury would help to solve a problem in this area. Since Mercury is called Budha in Vedic terminology, an image of the Buddha would also be a good idea. Alternatively, pictures of the sea or of marine animals could be used, or even an aquarium. In terms of décor, light blues are preferred in the western sector.

Light blue is associated with Mercury, the Regent Varuna and the West.

Light blue objects and décor are preferred in western sectors of the home.

A Problem in the Northwest

The northwest is a complex area, associated with both water and air. Its regent is Vayu, the wind-god, who inspires restlessness and distant communications. In planetary terms, the moon is the ruler of this quadrant, which makes it the perfect location for a bathroom or a guest bedroom. Permanence is not associated with the northwest so this is not a good area for a master bedroom, or indeed any room

AN INTRODUCTION TO VASTU

that is in regular use. Lunar symbols are the most appropriate appeasements here, and the image of a crescent moon will solve most of problems. This is also a good area for a telephone in order to enhance profitable communications. Soft, silvery tones and furnishings are recommended, as well as gentle blues and greens.

or for a kitchen or bathroom (a toilet here is said to flush one's wealth away). Images of high peaks, of gold and wealth are suitable appeasements to Kubera. Yellow is the colour of Jupiter in Vedic tradition, and a décor based on this should help to ensure good fortune.

Silvery objects and décor are lunar in character and provide a solution to problems in the Northwest.

Decorating your home office in yellow is a good idea since it promotes wealth.

A Problem in the North

The north is an area of health and wealth. In Vastu tradition it is governed by the prosperous Kubera, the diminutive dwarf-god of the Himalayas, and by the giant planet Jupiter. This is by far the best area for a study, office or library, and a good place to store valuables. It is not a good area for portraits of one's ancestors

Yellows and amber coloured objects are appropriate appeasements in the North.

A Problem in the Northeast

This is one of the most important areas of the home and is referred to as the gateway of the gods, the source of life-giving *prana*. Its regent is Soma, the moon-god, and personification of the elixir of eternal life. However, in Vastu astrology, this area is ruled by Surya the sun. The traditional use for this area is as a place to be

A musical instrument such as this Balinese flute would be a welcome addition to the Northeast.

56

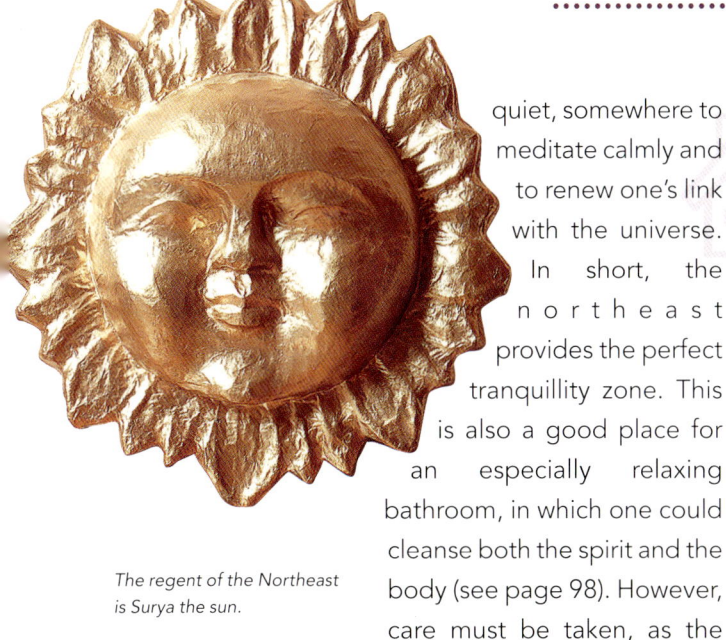

APPLYING VASTU

The regent of the Northeast is Surya the sun.

This area is the Gateway of the Gods and is primarily associated with the element of Aether.

quiet, somewhere to meditate calmly and to renew one's link with the universe. In short, the northeast provides the perfect tranquillity zone. This is also a good place for an especially relaxing bathroom, in which one could cleanse both the spirit and the body (see page 98). However, care must be taken, as the northeast is not really a place for bulky items such as baths. In fact, the northeast should always be kept as clear and minimalist as possible to allow Prana to flow freely into to the home. A front door located in this sector is particularly fortunate. Images of the sun and moon are suitable as are items that are gold or silver in colour. Aether is associated with sound, so a music centre, musical instruments or a wind chime would provide a suitable appeasement here.

A Problem in the Sacred Centre

This is the sector of the regent Brahma, the creator, and the element of aether or space. Ideally the centre of a home, and the centre of each room in the home, should be left unoccupied for inspirational and creative forces to be present in the lives of the occupants of the home. Problems such as heavy furniture or clutter in this central area may be solved by adding an image of Brahma himself (although the spiritual essence of a creator god from another religion would be equally as effective). Brahma's symbols of a lotus, a swan, a string of beads would be acceptable alternatives, as would a book with an uplifting theme. If using colour, adapt the décor with reddish hues. Aether does not have a symbolic image or a colour, but can be appeased with pleasing music or a wind chime.

An image of a swan (the mount of Brahma) would provide an appeasement for a problem in the sacred centre.

The colour red is particularly connected to the creator god.

AN INTRODUCTION TO VASTU

WORST-CASE SCENARIOS

The kitchen is located in the southwest quadrant – an earthy sector associated with the sign of Virgo and the goddess of sleep and ghosts, Nirriti. Ideally the kitchen needs to be in the southeast, governed by fire, the sign of Gemini, and Agni, the fire-god. The problem will only be solved with appeasements to the elements, earth and fire. (See pages 53-54: A Problem in the Southwest and A Problem in the Southeast.)

This oil burner is a perfect appeasement to Agni, particularly in view of the triangular features of its design.

Attractive, empty containers have the essence of the element of Aether.

A room is so small that there is no way of keeping the sacred centre free of clutter. This will inevitably lead to a lack of confidence, creativity and focus. An appeasement must be made either to Brahma or the element aether. (See page 57: A Problem in the Sacred Centre.)

A collection of attractive pebbles provides the appeasement to the Earth element.

The bathroom or w.c. is located in the northeast quadrant – the gateway of the gods. Although this is restful, this will ultimately lead to misfortune because of the fixed furniture blocking the flow of *prana*. An appeasement must be made to the elements aether and water. (See page 55, A Problem in the Northwest.)

Ornaments like this dolphin are emblems of the Water element.

Beads are a symbol of the creator god Brahma, they therefore provide an appeasement for the sacred centre.

58

APPLYING VASTU

A bedroom is located in the southeast – the area of Agni the fire-god. Worse still, a bed is in the southeast of the bedroom too. This is bound to cause sleepless nights, irritability and outbursts of anger. An appeasement to both water and fire is necessary in this room. (See page 53: A Problem in the Southeast.)

This yellow paperweight should be pleasing the Agni, since yellow is symbolic of fire.

The dolphin soap-dish provides the appeasement to the water element.

Your money is running low and you don't know where to turn. The answer to this lies in the northern sector of your home. This is the direction of Kubera, the dwarf-god of wealth. A good tip to improve your financial fortunes is to place a representation of the merciful goddess Lakshmi in the north together with a few coins as an appeasement to her and to Kubera (who is said to particularly enjoy her company). The north is also the best place for a safe or security box. In order to maintain wealth that you have already, place a statuette of Lakshmi in the safe with your valuables.

The best place for a safe, security box or even a bottle with pennies in it is in the North, the area of wealth.

A statuette of Lakshmi placed in a safe is said to ensure continued prosperity.

CASE STUDIES

Throughout this book we have used an ordinary suburban home as an example of how the ancient arts of Vastu can be easily combined with the necessities of modern living. Vastu principles are easy to apply once you have an idea of the directions and the usage of each room within the home. In most cases no major alteration need be done, but an eye for the appropriate detail here and there can transform the atmosphere of any living space into something positive and uplifting through the correct application of Vastu.

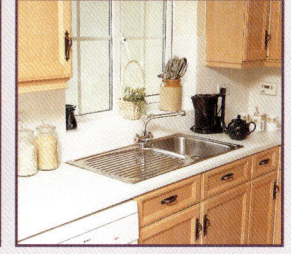

THE ENTRANCE TO YOUR HOME

IN VASTU, the entrance to the home is associated with notions of respect and public status.

The front door, or mainly used entrance to your home is symbolic of public recognition and status. Accord to Vastu, this doorway should be attractive and the pathway leading to it, should be free of obstructions unless it faces Southwest. In this case some overhanging bushes are a good idea to discourage negative forces from entering the home.

THE PATH

If there is a path leading up to the entrance of a home, there should be no obstructions on it. Overhanging plants should be cut back so that healthful *prana* can flow freely to the front door.

A path that is located in the northeast signifies good fortune for the inhabitants of the home. It should therefore be as wide and spacious as possible to maximise the *prana* flowing to the gateway of the gods. The opposite is true of path or entrance located in the southwest. This is an area of negative energy, harmful to health and luck. Here, a pathway should be narrow and meandering. Overhanging bushes are to be encouraged, as their very life force will discourage the bad vibes of the southwest.

Having to mount steps to enter a dwelling is considered good in Vastu. This rustic entrance with its clear entryway and three steps is very fortunate.

60

THE ENTRANCE TO YOUR HOME

This long, unobstructed path faces north and it therefore very fortuitous.

The slightly overgrown borders of this path will decrease the negativity of the Southwest.

An uneven number of steps leading to the front door increases the luck of the household.

According to the *trigunas* square (see page 17), your home is governed by three positive and negative universal forces. A doorway in the north, northeast or east falls under the *sattva* force, and is considered very fortunate physically, spiritually and in terms of personal wealth. This is also true of an entrance in the *rajas* sections, therefore the northwest and southeast. An entrance in the *tamas*-governed southwest, on the other hand, is most unfortunate, and an appeasement to the earth element, the planet Saturn or the regent Nirriti will be necessary for happiness to enter your home (see page 54).

Other physical features relating to the approach to a house require attention. For example, a road that points straight at your property is said to endanger the inhabitants. If you live at the end of a cul-de-sac or on a T-junction, therefore, this is a portent of misfortune. Living at the centre of a crossroads is unlucky too. Equally, a front door that opens onto a road that runs north-south, along the fire line, denotes money troubles. Each of these problems can be solved by choosing a suitable appeasement to the element, regent or planet associated with the directions involved.

AN INTRODUCTION TO VASTU

THE FRONT DOOR

The main entrance is regarded as the mouth of Purusha in Vastu (see page 12). It is important that it be sufficiently wide (21/2 feet/0.75m) and adequately tall (6 feet/2m).

The front door is regarded as the "mouth" of the house.

A door that opens in a clockwise direction is more fortunate than one which opens anticlockwise. The front door itself should be solid, implying security in the home. Glass should be kept to a minimum, unless you want your family's secrets and private affairs to be revealed to the world. A noisy door, for example, one that creaks or is prone to slamming is not desirable feature, as it harms the *prana* entering the home and

A transparent front door is not a good idea because family secrets will be revealed to the world.

A solid front door, set back in good surroundings implies security and happiness.

implies that the owner of the property is not in control of his or her own affairs. A doorway that is below ground level, as in the case of basement apartments, is a disadvantage, and can be remedied by directing a light up the door to dispel evil influences.

Many traditional houses in southern India have a raised threshold just outside the main door. The purpose of this is to ensure that visitors to the home have to bow when entering, thereby symbolically honouring the regent, direction and element of the doorway. Many entrances to Indian homes are colourfully and intricately decorated with motifs of flowers, birds, shells, images of gods and auspicious Sanskrit phrases, and some decoration around the

THE ENTRANCE TO YOUR HOME

This is just about the maximum amount of glass to be permitted in a front door. Stained, or otherwise patterned glass should be considered a beneficial feature.

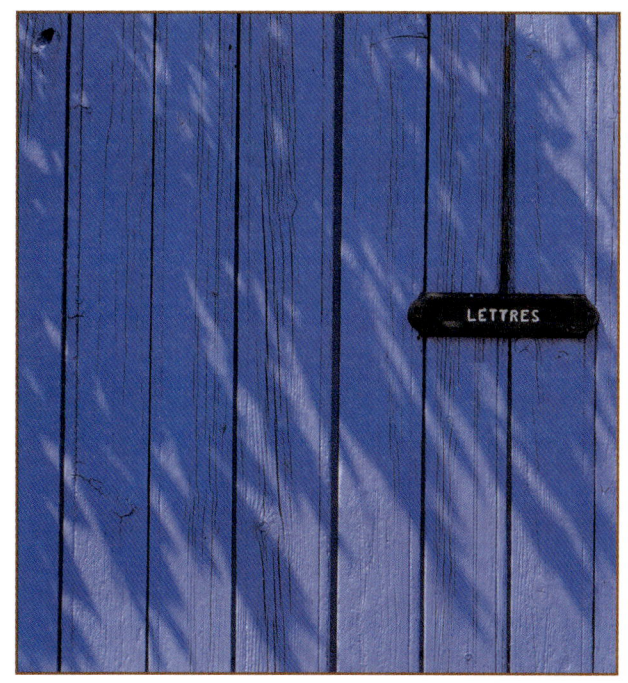

A door such as this, solid and traditional implies self-reliance and a sense of heritage.

An image of the beautiful goddess Lakshmi or the genial elephant-headed god Ganesha placed in close proximity to the front door will enhance positive energy and dispel negativity from this region.

The genial, elephant-headed god Ganesha placed near the front door is considered to be very fortunate indeed.

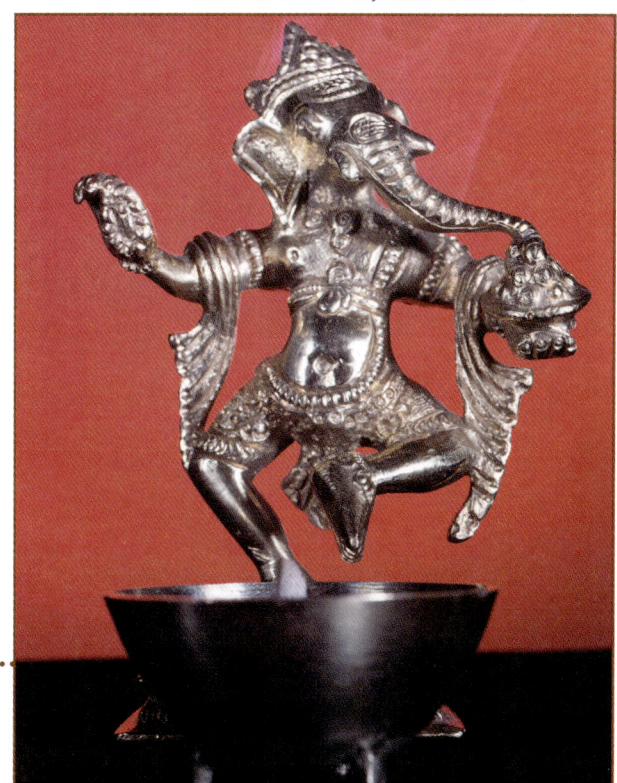

doorway is considered to be beneficial. However, some images should be avoided, such as anything that hints at war and battle, fierce animals and nude or erotic figures.

AN INTRODUCTION TO VASTU

THE HALLWAY

The fundamental Vastu requirement for a hallway or foyer is that it be light and airy, with enough space for two people to pass each other comfortably. In terms of décor, the colour scheme of the hallway should be dictated either by the regent or direction of the front door. If the latter happens to be the southwest, colours that can act as an appeasement are best. They are most likely to be the colours associated with the north or the northeast, namely yellow or light blue.

Hallways should be light and airy. Its décor dictated by the direction of the front door. A Northwest facing door would suggest a hallway decorated with light blues and greens. A hallway facing Southeast on the other hand would be ideally painted yellow.

STAIRWAYS

Many hallways have a stairwell rising from them, and the general rule here is that they will be more fortunate if they possess an odd, rather than even, number of steps, and particularly if, when the number of the steps is divided by three, there is a remainder of two. Therefore, stairs that have eleven, thirteen or seventeen steps are considered to be the best and most fortunate.

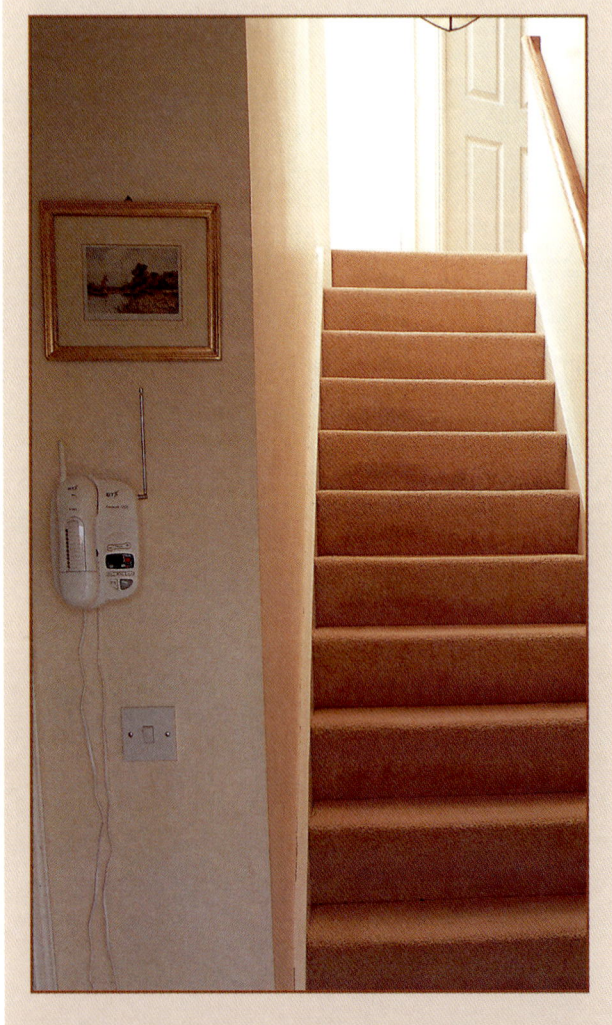

Stairways with an odd rather than an even number of steps are considered to be very fortunate. This is especially true if the steps number eleven, thirteen or seventeen. In this case there are eleven stairs, a particularly good feature in this house.

THE ENTRANCE TO YOUR HOME

Solid rather than open steps are to be preferred in Vastu. Open stairs suggest fragility and anxiety while a continuous stairway enhances prosperity.

Long, narrow stairs or those with gaps between each step are unfortunate because they represent a loss of vitality, fragile health and money worries. In an ideal situation stairs should be wide, gently curving (preferably to the right) and located in the southwest of a home or room.

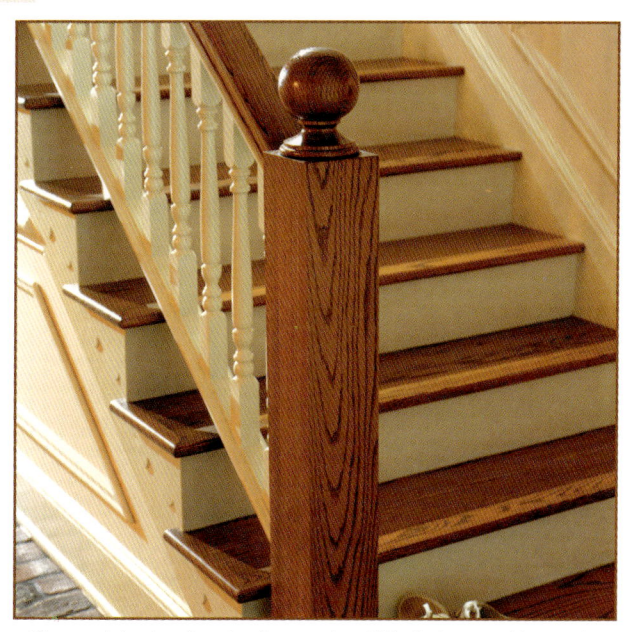

The sturdy banister here implies security within the home, adding to the fortunate number of steps in this stairway.

INTERNAL DOORS

The general rule regarding a noisy front door applies to internal doors as well. Vastu tradition also states that a home will be more fortunate if it has an even, rather than odd, number of doors within it.

A solid banister would provide an added sense of security in this home, while a wide spacious stairwell in the other is very fortunate.

Stairs that curve in a clockwise direction are considered to be more fortunate than those that don't. However, stairs that are situated in the northeast or the sacred centre of a home require extensive appeasements, as neither of these areas will enhance luck. Stairs located directly opposite a main entrance also require an appeasement, as do those that are above a bedroom.

Creaking doors imply a loss of control as does a cluttered coat rail tucked away behind a door. Homes are considered more fortunate if there is an even rather than odd number of doors within it.

THE LIVING ROOM

The heavy bookcase and bulky sofa are best placed in the Southwest where their mass will serve as a barrier against the negative influence of that direction.

THE IDEAL LIVING room should be comfortable and welcoming. It is a place to relax and to feel at ease. Those who live within the home, and those who visit, should feel that this room is an extension of the personality of the occupants. Visitors should enjoy being in your space as much as they enjoy your company. Fundamentally, this room should be informal, even if you prefer a fairly austere décor, with great emotional warmth.

In many ways the lounge, living room or family room is the most important area in the home. It is the area of socialising, where one's friends are entertained, as well as being a place for the family gather together. It is also the place where many treasured mementos are on display.

PICTURE PLACEMENT

Photographs and family souvenirs should be displayed according to age. The best place for pictures of older generations is in the north – the direction of wellbeing and prosperity. Photographs of those who have passed on should be displayed in the south – the direction of Yama, lord of the afterlife. Children's pictures are best placed in the east – the direction of youth and exuberance.

The placement of family photographs is important. Those of children should be placed in the East while images of departed relatives should be positioned in the South.

THE CYCLE OF LIFE

Life is a major function of the living room and, therefore, the rhythm of existence – the past, present and future – should be represented in some way. If

THE LIVING ROOM

In all homes it is important that the central space or sacred centre should be empty of furniture and free of clutter.

Traditional Indian homes are often constructed around a central courtyard, the interaction between inside and outside being less pronounced in a warm climate. Even so, in these homes, the area that we would term a living room is usually to the north of this central courtyard area.

THE SACRED CENTRE

In the symbolic language of Vastu, the living room represents the heart of the home, with the centre of the room as its soul. The central courtyard in traditional Indian homes is often kept empty as it is thought of as the place of Brahma the creator and

your living room is old fashioned and amply furnished with antiques, a modern touch should be introduced to symbolise the future. The reverse is also true. The most contemporary designs will benefit from the presence of something older, representing tradition.

The sacred centre is the place of the regent Brahma, the creator-god. For this reason it is considered to be the most holy part of the home. It is the heart of a home and therefore any clutter here will strike at the very heart of the family. Keep this space clear of clutter and good fortune will attend your house.

Modern surroundings would benefit from a hint of the traditional to ensure continuity, while more old-fashioned rooms need a touch of the modern to ensure progress.

Ideally this focus of activity should be located in one of the three northerly sections of the home. The northwest, the north and the northeast are the favoured directions for a major living space. However, do not lose sight of the fact that it is also advantageous to have a large portion of the living room in the central or sacred zone of the home.

therefore the most holy place in the property. For this reason, it is never a good idea to position an occasional table in the middle of a living room, especially if the table is groaning with ashtrays, plates, crumpled magazines and half-drained coffee cups. In short, the centre of anything is sacred and should therefore be kept empty. If you must have a small table in the living room, try to position it off-centre so that the place of Brahma retains its holiness and continues to bestow its blessings.

AN INTRODUCTION TO VASTU

Even though this fireplace is for visual effect only its position in the area of Agni and fire in the Southeast is apt. The metal fireguard also serves as an attractive candle-holder so is both an appeasement to Mars and to the fire element.

Agni needs no appeasement in this living room where a real fire expresses the joy of the flame-god.

A ROOM TO PARTY

If you are a social animal and like to entertain on a weekly basis, then a living room located in the northwest is ideal – governed by the planet Mercury, which symbolises animated and amusing conversation and, perhaps more importantly, by the regent Vayu, representing the wind. (Vayu also represents action and movement, so late guests will naturally feel a little restless in this area and will not outstay their welcome.) The décor for a northwesterly living room should include yellow to stimulate conversation and laughter.

A light and airy sitting room encourages relaxation especially if it is positioned in the northerly part of the home.

THE LIVING ROOM

A party atmosphere in the living room will be enhanced if yellow is used in the decor. This colour stimulates laughter and conversation.

A ROOM FOR QUIET CONTEMPLATION

If you prefer a quiet life, your living room is ideally situated in the northeastern segment of your home. This area relates to the watery element and is the source of positive *prana*. The result is happiness, a sense of tranquillity and the perfect area in which to unwind after a particularly hard day. A living room with a northeasterly aspect is especially suitable for someone who enjoys reading and listening to relaxing music. It is the sort of area where the troubles of the outside world melt away. In this sense, a living room in the northeast serves as a tranquillity zone in its own right. The colour scheme for a northeastern living room should include light blues and greens to enhance relaxation.

THE BEST OF BOTH WORLDS

If you consider yourself neither an extrovert nor an introvert, then the best place for your living room is in the north. This position can be described as the best of both worlds because a living room here falls under the auspices of the dwarf regent, Kubera, the self-indulgent bestower of wealth, the optimistic and exuberant planet Jupiter and Soma the god of health. In short a living room with a northern aspect creates wholesome vibrations which will be felt by anyone who spends time in this room. This space is social enough for entertaining but will also provide an atmosphere of calm when you are alone. This is also a good position for a sitting-room-cum-library on account of the influence of Jupiter or Guru, the planet of study and learning. The décor of a northerly living room is not specified but yellows, greens and light blues will be favoured here.

A bookcase in the living room brings in the influence of Guru or the planet Jupiter as the guardian of knowledge. Although the traditional place for books is the North a bookcase may also be used as a barrier against negativity in the Southwest.

ARRANGING THE FURNITURE

It is important that a living room does not become cluttered with furniture that does not serve a specific purpose. An over-stuffed room is very off-putting and can be oppressive to both those who live in the home and those who visit. A living room should be light and airy, giving people room to breathe, both physically and metaphorically.

Heavy items of furniture should be placed in the Southwest if possible.

Wherever possible features of the natural world should be included in your décor. This basket of pine-cones for instance symbolically creates an aura of woodland calm within the living area.

It is a good idea to bring the natural world into the living area by including healthy plants, attractive stones, clay pots and wooden furniture. The natural world may also be represented through scenic images or photographs.

An arrangement of healthy plants and clay pots reminds us of our links to the earth.

Wooden furniture is to be preferred to plastics because it is a product of the natural world.

The most important items of furniture in a living room are the sofa and chairs, which tend to be heavy and bulky. If your personal home geography permits they should be sited in either the south or the west. This ensures that when seated one either faces the north – the direction of blessings, health and wealth, or to the east – the direction of vitality, love and enthusiasm. Remember to keep furniture at least 10cm (4in) from the nearest wall.

THE LIVING ROOM

This is a harmonious arrangement of features combining the natural wooden elements of the fireplace and the mirror surround, with fire features (the fireplace again) such as candles as well as a mirror which is a lunar influence encouraging self-knowledge and enlightened attitudes.

Seating areas should not be directly in front of doors or windows, as this will lead to negative undercurrents within the family and subconscious feelings of anxiety. Those who habitually sit with their backs to a window or door will find that family quarrels are inevitable because no one will feel secure deep down and this leads to friction.

TELEVISION, TELEPHONE AND ENTERTAINMENT CENTRES

Electricity and electrical items get hot and are considered to be fiery in nature. They therefore properly belong to Agni the lord of fire, and should be sited in the southeast of the room. An exception to this rule applies when you feel that entertainment is taking up too much of your family's time and attention. Placing a television in the northwest corner of the room, for example, will lead to a sense of restlessness and enable you to turn the set off more readily.

The best position for the television is either in the Southeast, the fire-direction relating to electricity or, if your viewing habits are too extensive, in the Northwest. The restlessness of this area will encourage you to get up and do something else.

Similarly, welcome news and entertaining chats will be encouraged if the telephone is located in the beneficial northwestern segment of the living room, unless this is your preferred tranquillity zone. In this case, the phone may be placed anywhere in the living room but the plug point should remain in this area. The northwest is particularly good for communication, its planetary governor being Mercury or Budha.

The telephone is best placed in the Northwest, the area of Vayu the wind-god and Budha or Mercury. This placement encourages pleasing and profitable news.

Radios and other electronic equipment are best placed in the Southeast, the area of Agni, regent of fire.

CABINETS, CUPBOARDS AND SHELVES

The southern and westerly directions are important in the positioning of other heavy items of furniture such as china cabinets, sideboards and bookshelves. Remember that the southwest itself is the source of the negative energies associated with Nirriti, the

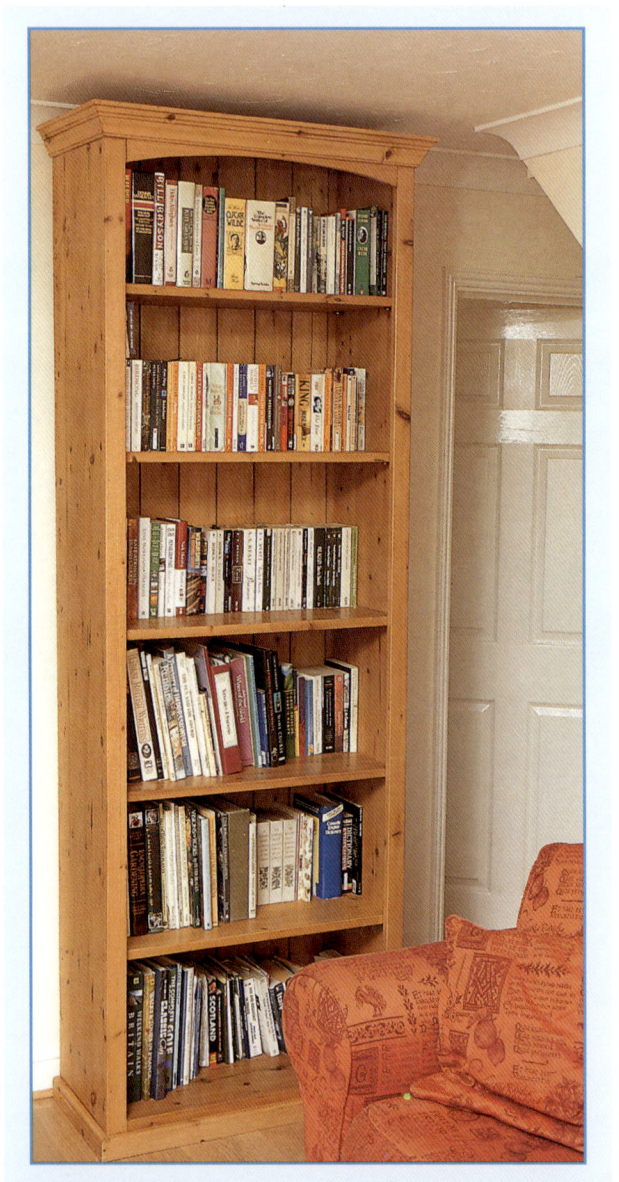

By far the best position for heavy furniture is the Southwest where it can act as a barrier to negativity. However you may place a bookcase in the North, governed by Jupiter guardian of knowledge if you prefer.

THE LIVING ROOM

Books have two symbolic functions in Vastu. Firstly as the repositories of knowledge there are governed by Jupiter. If these books are of an uplifting or religious nature then they are associated with the sacred centre and Brahma the creator.

The same remedy might be tried with other heavy items such as large cupboards or storage chests. However, visual balance is just as important ingredient in planning a living room so there avoid an imbalance of heavy furnishings directed here. Heavy furniture is permitted in any part of the room (except the sacred centre and the beneficial northwest) especially if it adds to an overall sense of symmetry.

goddess of nightmares, so large obstacles to these unfortunate influences are advantageous. Some Vastu practitioners advise that, if you are an insatiable reader, your weightiest books should be kept on a built-in bookshelf near the southwest corner of the lounge. The shelves and the books on them will then serve as a barrier against the ill-fortune emanating from the southwest.

This image of Nirriti on her lion appeases the goddess of nightmares when placed in the Southwest.

This triangular cabinet is symbolically related to the fire element (the symbolic shape of fire being the triangle) it should therefore be placed in the Southeast.

AN INTRODUCTION TO VASTU

THE TRANQUILLITY ZONE

Zones of tranquillity are important in every room of the house and, in particular in the living room. Of course, if the living room is in the northwest portion of your home it will already serve as a serene area, suitable for contemplation and relaxation. Should the living room be in any other area of your home, however, you should create a little tranquil zone within the room. As usual, the ideal place for this is in the northwest corner – always the best location for your favourite chair. Another option is to create this peaceful spot near a fireplace, especially one with a living flame. The flickering light of a comforting blaze can help to soothe troubled thoughts.

Comfort and peace are the main requirements of the tranquillity zone so a comfortable chair in which to sit and ponder the world is a bonus.

The influence of nature should also be felt in the tranquil zone. Some healthy, bushy plants would be a welcome addition to here, as indeed would anything tactile such as a bowl of pebbles or shells. This would be a good position for an aquarium, a mobile or wind chime – anything that has gentle motion. In some traditional Indian homes this is the place for a swing or hammock. If you don't want to go that far, a rocking chair wouldn't be a bad idea.

Anything tactile like a bowl of pebbles or shells is a good idea in this serene area.

Every room in the home should have its own tranquillity zone. This does not have to be anything spectacular even though in India this zone often includes a shrine of some kind. All that is required is a comfortable chair, a pleasant atmosphere and some peace in which to enjoy your time there.

THE LIVING ROOM

A good old-fashioned rocking chair is perfect for a tranquillity zone in a traditional home.

bulb dangling centrally from the ceiling. This will serve to highlight every imperfection in both the room and those who occupy it. Always invest in an attractive lampshade that is in keeping with the room's décor. It is an even better idea to have a number of attractive table lamps scattered about the living room, creating a welcoming ambience. An uplight is a good investment, too, especially if you read a lot. An excellent place for this sort of lamp is in the tranquillity zone.

The atmospheric use of candles can be a mood enhancer.

A hammock can be so relaxing that you might not want to leave it.

An attractive lampshade in keeping with the room's décor adds to the peaceful ambience.

MOOD LIGHTING

The issue of lighting is especially important in the living room. The worst-case scenario is a single bare

You should always pay attention to the lighting especially in the tranquillity zone.

75

THE DINING AREA

It is important that when dining you should not sit with your back to a window or door as this will lead to subconscious feelings of insecurity and add to underlying tensions within the family.

THERE IS SOME leeway in the placement of the dining area. Traditionally it should be located either in the east or the west of your home. It is sensible that this room should also be in close proximity to the kitchen. (If your dining area is in the kitchen, it should be to the west of the room. Bear in mind that Vastu teaching insists that combining the kitchen and dining area is undesirable because cooking and eating are incompatible in elemental terms. In this case, the two portions should be clearly defined, psychologically creating two rooms out of one as it were. A screen of some sort might help, as indeed would a subtle change of décor between the two areas.

A screen can help to psychologically create two rooms out of one.

When sitting at a table in the dining room, one should face either east or west. Facing west is said to enhance one's chances of prosperity while facing east claims to promote health and lead to a long life. If neither of these options are possible then it is just acceptable to face south when eating, but facing north should always be avoided.

THE DINING AREA

THE SHAPE OF THE TABLE

The most important feature of the dining area is the table. Vastu maintains that a circular or oval table will create an abundance of positive energy, adding to the goodness that is ingested with the food. This sort of table is also said to create the right sort of atmosphere for family communication and entertaining conversation at mealtimes.

In its most traditional form, Vastu aims to avoid an overly animated conversation over dinner. Instead, it stresses the importance of sitting quietly while absorbing nutrition. After all, modern habits of eating fast food are not good for the internal balance of our bodies or the serenity of our minds, so it would do us no harm at all to slow down and have a decent meal according to Vastu tradition once in a while. If you crave an atmosphere of calm while you eat, then a square or rectangular table is recommended, and that you sit facing west.

A circular or oval table creates the right atmosphere for open communication within the family.

THE SACRED CENTRE

The dining table should not be placed in the exact centre of the room, as the energies of the sacred central space could become imprisoned beneath the table or between the feet of the sitters. Instead, position the table either to the east or west of the central point, depending on your particular

The narrow plan of this dining room ensures that the table occupies the middle of the space, thereby offending Brahma and the sacred centre. One chair also backs onto a window. Future problems can be avoided if there is an appeasement to Brahma and the chair moved from such a vulnerable position.

preference. If the table inclines to the east, a more stimulating, conversational atmosphere will be created. If to the west, a quieter, more tranquil mealtime will be achieved.

The attractive plain glass bowl is a suitable appeasement to the sacred centre as long as it is kept empty and in the middle of the table. In this way the idea of a void is maintained at the centre.

AN INTRODUCTION TO VASTU

FURNISHINGS

China cabinets, Welsh dressers, sideboards and other large items should be positioned at the south or west walls, following the general guideline that they should be placed at least 10cm (4in) from the walls.

The Welsh dresser should be moved to at least four inches from the wall to allow prana to flow past it. It is wise to position such large items of furniture near the western or southern walls of the room.

Perishable items and goods such as fruit bowls, flowers, and even the wine rack, should be kept in the northern portion of the room – the place of treasures, governed by the regent Kubera and the planet Jupiter. It is said that the energies of the north will help preserve that which can decay and maintain your perishable items for a longer period. In the case of wine, the northern energies will increase its bouquet and potency.

Wine should traditionally be kept in the northern portion of the room especially if you want it to mature into a fine vintage.

THE MOOD OF THE ROOM

Many people like the dining area to be a formal space with a strict order of seating. Care must be taken, however, to avoid a tension in the environment at mealtimes, which may cause inner anxieties and digestive problems among the diners. Instead, mealtimes are supposed to calm the soul as the body takes in nourishment. To create an air of serenity, the walls of the dining room should be painted in a gentle colour, preferably light blue or soft green. Loud wallpaper and discordant colours anywhere in the room should be avoided.

One of the most difficult issues in the dining area is that of lighting. If it is too bright there may be an aura of strict formality, and an exaggeration of any imperfections in the room. Soft, understated lighting is preferred here, and the simple installation of a dimmer switch will help to create a more positive and intimate mood at evening meals. Candles may be used to add a touch of romance.

THE DINING AREA

Soft furnishings for this area should reflect the subtle interplay of light and shadow in the room. The colour green will promote harmony and wellbeing, but should not be too dark or gloomy. Dark, heavy fabrics will create a feeling of tension and formality, while light, airy fabrics will enhance the mood and create a more friendly, welcoming atmosphere.

A mirror here is not such a good idea. Mirrors by nature are reflective and encourage self-questioning. In a dining room attention should be focused on one's meal firstly, and secondly on those in your company. Examination of the inner workings of your psyche is not an activity for mealtimes.

It is always a good idea to include the natural world in one's décor. Healthy plants are always a bonus.

Candles can provide a relaxing atmosphere at meal times.

Vastu tradition also suggests that fabrics should be used in combination with more sturdy materials, for example, with wood and metal. Delicate wrought iron can be used to represents the element of air. Upholstery should have a natural theme in its patterning and should complement the soft furnishings of the tranquillity zone. It is a good idea to include at least two tall, healthy plants in your dining room.

AN INTRODUCTION TO VASTU

This wrought iron chair is suggestive of natural forms so is acceptable but it would still be better to invest in wooden furniture.

Using flowers as a centrepiece breathes life into the dining area.

Placing a fruit bowl, amply supplied with fresh fruits, as a centrepiece for the table or in the northern section of the room will promise abundance. In Vedic belief, the fruits of the earth represent prosperity, and their presence in the dining room will bring luck to the home. If fresh fruits are lacking, a picture of them somewhere in the dining room, preferably on the north wall, will have the same fortunate effects.

A fruit bowl as a table centrepiece is a good idea as long as the table doesn't occupy the middle of the room. Placing a fruit bowl in the North promises abundance.

In many traditional homes family photographs are often displayed in the dining room. However, care should be taken that pictures of the deceased should be placed in the south and southwest, because these areas relate to the afterlife and to one's ancestors.

THE DINING AREA

THE TRANQUILLITY ZONE

It is recommended that a tranquillity zone should be included in your dining room décor, and that it should be placed in the north, northeast or eastern segments of the room. A soft chair or padded bench may be placed here together with an attractive side table and

Any chair used for the tranquillity zone should be light and softly padded.

A soft chair or padded bench can be used as a tranquillity zone in the dining area.

any items of sentimental value that you treasure. If you only little space to spare, perhaps a single item of spiritual significance could be placed here instead. Vastu tradition suggests that a sprig of basil (sacred to the great god Vishnu, the preserver) is a good idea, and will promote harmony of mind and body. Another possibilty is to hang a picture of someone whose ideals you respect as a reminder of the more worthy virtues of which humanity is capable.

A pleasant, serene view from the dining area is considered a bonus in Vastu.

THE KITCHEN

THIS IS ONE of the most important rooms in the home and Vastu guidelines for the kitchen aim to make this a room in which we are happy to spend time, taking the necessary trouble to prepare meals in an atmosphere of calm serenity.

According to Vedic teaching, we take in spiritual as well as physical nourishment when we eat but, in these times of fast food and convenience meals, the spiritual quality can often be lacking. It is doubly important, therefore, that when we do prepare a meal at home, we do so in a correctly oriented kitchen.

The kitchen has a lot of metal implements and heat in it. It is therefore apt that it is associated with fiery Mars and hot-blooded Agni.

The oven, hob, and microwave should ideally be positioned in the South-eastern portion of the kitchen. If this is not an easy matter then a suitable appeasement should be made to the fire element and to the element or regent of the direction the heat generating appliance is actually in.

THE KITCHEN

LOCATION, LOCATION, LOCATION

The best placement for the kitchen is in the southeastern sector of the home. This is the fire area, sacred to Agni, and associated with Mars or Kuja. The presence of the god of war in this area may at first seem strange, yet it is logical when one considers the presence of so many sharp implements such as carving knives, and heat sources such as the oven hob.

Although the southeast is the preferred sector for the kitchen, this room is not easily relocated within the home. Fortunately this rule need only be taken as a guideline, as there are other ways of making the kitchen harmonious. Firstly, the kitchen should be some distance from the main entrance to your home. This will avoid bad luck and negative energies contaminating one's food. It is equally important that the kitchen be well lit and well ventilated. Finally, in an ideal situation, the kitchen should be located on the ground floor of a dwelling.

The sink, dishwasher, washing machine and kettle are ideally placed in the East, Northeast or Southwest. The sink particularly should be positioned against the eastern or northern wall. The view from the window above the sink could conceivably serve as a tranquillity zone in this often busy area of the home.

It is only in relatively recent times that kitchens have included a water source, and certainly Vedic law would not have taken this into consideration. This presence of water alters the elemental balance of the kitchen, and consequently another suitable location for food preparation area is the northeast. This sector is associated with Soma the moon-god who brews the elixir of eternal life, and is also known as the gateway of the gods because it is from here that *prana*, the breath of life flows. Further symbolism involves the concept of motherhood and nurturing, and therefore caring for the family.

The presence of knives and sharp metallic objects in the kitchen is a reminder that this area comes under the rulership of Mars.

If you consider yourself to have a particularly 'fiery' personality, or think that your family is volatile in nature, then the northeast is preferable to the southeast. This is because the watery nature of this direction will tend to douse the flames of excitable family members. The northwest is also an acceptable position for the kitchen because this is one of the areas that are favourable to your fortunes. However if your kitchen is in this sector of the home, you should face east while preparing your meals.

AN INTRODUCTION TO VASTU

It is never a good idea to site your kitchen in the southwest – the ill-omened sector of Nirriti and her demons. It is said that heat naturally resides here, and so adding the warmth of a kitchen would create too much heat for comfort. If the kitchen occupies part of the home that is neither in the southeast or northeast, then a suitable appeasement must be found to guarantee good health and prosperity. If the kitchen is in the southwest in particular, an appeasement must be found that will maintain the luck of the household.

Should the kitchen occupy any area other than the Northeast or Southeast then an appeasement must be made both to the fire element and the force of the direction the kitchen is actually in. If for instance the kitchen were in the Northwest it might be safest to make appeasements to fire, water and air. A wind-chime would serve for air, candles or triangular objects for fire and a mirror, a crescent or even a picture of a fish would serve for water.

PREPARING A MEAL

Preferably, one should face east when preparing food for cooking – the early rays of the sun are said to add goodness to the ingredients – as the blessings of mighty Indra and of Surya the sun-god will shower upon you and your family. Facing south while cooking is said to invite troubles to women of the family, while facing west is said to cause bone ailments or bad complexions. Facing north while preparing food should always be avoided, since this invites debt problems and financial worries.

Spices have always been a major ingredient in Indian

Ideally one should face east when preparing the ingredients of a meal.

cuisine. Their fragrance is not only appetising, but has a role to play in the perfect Vastu kitchen. The wholesome odours of ginger, basil, cinnamon, cardamom, nutmeg and coriander have a positive bearing on health as well as adding a tasty piquancy

Fragrant spices have an important role in a Vastu kitchen.

84

THE KITCHEN

to one's food. Many of these spices have medicinal virtues and can also be used in teas or as herbal infusions. At the very least, they can help the digestive process and therefore remove the basic causes of many disorders. Garlic is another very beneficial vegetable. It not only keeps vampires at bay, but also purifies the blood and can relieve the symptoms of coughs and colds. A string of garlic bulbs can be used as a decorative feature when hung from a kitchen ceiling. It is a good idea to feature these ingredients in a Vastu kitchen, simply by using a spice rack. Alternatively, consider growing little herbs and spices in pots on a sunny windowsill.

The perfect place for all electrical appliances is the Southeast. If items such as the microwave oven is anywhere else then you may have to consider an appeasement to fire and to the element that governs the area the appliance is in.

The sink should be against the northern or eastern wall. The refrigerator – a typically heavy kitchen appliance – can be placed in the southwest as a barrier against negative forces. Failing this, the north

An attractive arrangement of herbs brings nature into the kitchen as well as adding a tasty piquancy to food.

KITCHEN APPLIANCES

In the ideal Vastu kitchen, stoves, hobs, microwave ovens – anything that radiates heat – should be positioned in the southeastern part of the room. Appliances that use water – washing machine, dishwasher, kettle – should be placed in the east, northeast or southwest.

The sink is best placed in a watery or aetheric area such as the Northwest or Northeast.

or the west are also good places for the fridge, particularly the west where wholesomeness can be added to the food from east as the door is opened.

A washing machine is very heavy so it may be positioned in the Southwest to act as a barrier against negativity.

There should be some form of contrast between an eating area and a cooking area. A breakfast bar is acceptable but it should not jut out into the centre of the room.

A breakfast bar is an acceptable alternative to a dining table as long as it does not jut out into the centre of the room. Stools at the breakfast bar should face east or west, preferably. Facing south is acceptable but one should never face north when eating.

Cupboards and fitted units are best placed along the

FURNITURE PLACEMENT

If your kitchen is big enough, some part of it may also serve as a small breakfast or dining area, perhaps with a small table and chairs. It is important that the table does not occupy the exact centre of the room – the sacred centre – as it is vital that the positive energies of this space are free to radiate to the rest of the room. Any table in the kitchen should be square or rectangular, which will encourage leisurely eating. An easterly orientation for the table will also be beneficial, encouraging the healthful energies of the sun to improve the quality of the food and add to its spiritual nourishment.

It should be remembered that the two activities of cooking food and eating it are not compatible according to Vastu guidelines. If there is a dining area in the kitchen, therefore, some form of separation of the two areas is required. For example, a screen could be used, creating another room as it were. A subtle change in décor would also serve to create a contrast between the two areas.

Remember that any small, dark, enclosed space is the realm of gloomy Saturn. That is why extra effort should be made to brighten such an area up as well as keeping it free of clutter. It's best if you keep Saturn in the home to an absolute minimum.

THE KITCHEN

southern and western walls, ideally so that they meet neatly at the southwestern corner of the room, where they can act as a barrier against the negative forces of the southwest. As is usual in Vastu all furniture, apart from items that are fixed to the wall, should be at least 10cm (4in) from the wall.

THE TRANQUILLITY ZONE

A tranquillity zone is less important in the kitchen than in other rooms of the house, although it is good to have one small area of calm to focus on from time to time, perhaps a windowsill or a work top or small shelf set apart from your usual work area. Tradition suggests that an image of one of the beneficial deities will bring good fortune here. Hindus tend to prefer a statuette or picture of the jovial elephant-headed god Ganesha and his rat of prosperity, while Buddhists like an image of the Buddha. One could express an element of an alternative faith in this zone, for example, a Catholic might choose a crucifix or a rosary, and a Protestant may prefer a meaningful passage from the Bible. Concentrating on a personal belief is a good idea so that you might find your faith is reinforced as you look up during some repetitive activity such as chopping vegetables, and you will be re-energised by the power represented here. In short, the kitchen tranquillity zone should provide you with a reinvigorating meditative moment to help you through your day.

For many people the only hope of having a tranquil moment in the kitchen is the odd pause to gaze out of the window. If you have a good view from the kitchen this is excellent, if you do not then consider a window box or growing herbs in pots of the windowsill. Just one small area of calm in a hectic space is all it takes.

This serene garden area has a strong influence on the kitchen of our case study house. It provides a zone of tranquillity for a busy mum who has lots to do.

Oriental items such as this Buddhist prayer wheel (standing for aether) or this rather grotesque incense burner (standing for fire) would be excellent appeasements for a kitchen in the Northeast.

BEDROOMS

ALL BEDROOMS FALL under the influence of the planet Venus or Shukra, no matter where they happen to be in the home, or who sleeps there. Although it is well known that Venus is devoted to the pleasures of making love, the planet is no less concerned with nurturing the young, and with comfort, hospitality and prosperity.

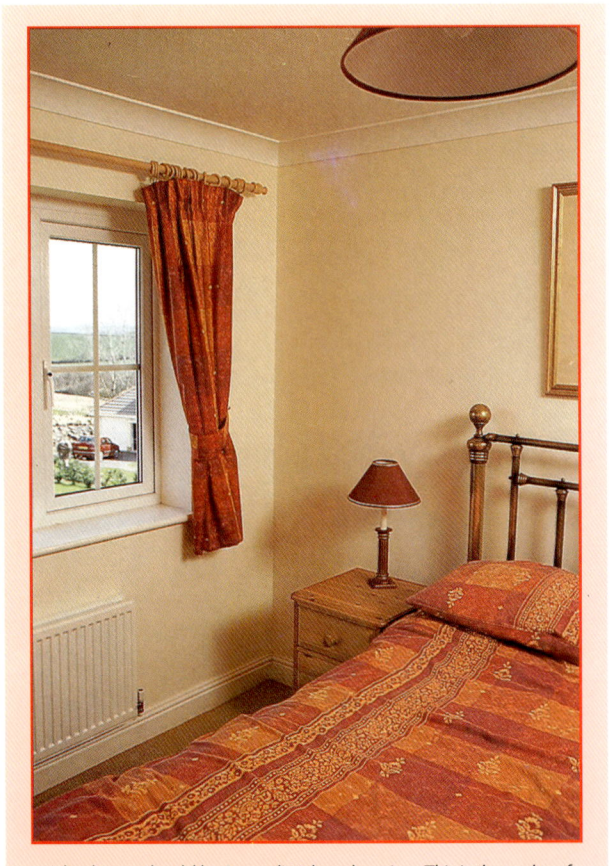

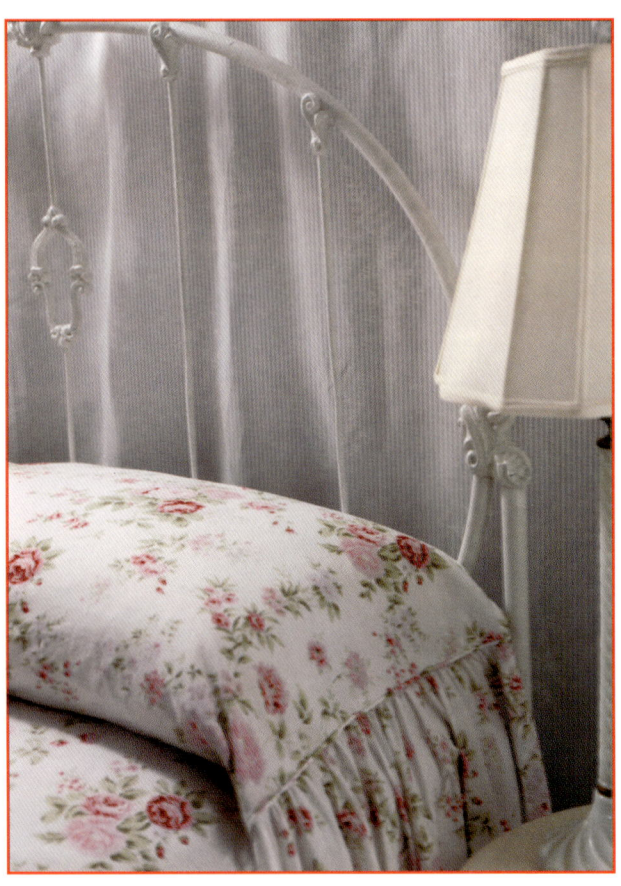

Big cushions and pillows, softness and the occasional hint of femininity appeal to the energies of Venus, although metal bedsteads are not so welcome.

A bedroom should be immediately welcoming. This is the realm of Venus, planet of love and an intimate atmosphere should be encouraged in this, the most private part of the home.

LOCATION, LOCATION, LOCATION

Ask yourself if you are happy with the way to your bedroom looks or feels. If you experience a constant desire to redecorate or rearrange the furniture, then some deep, intuitive part of you is trying to tell you to relocate to another area of the home.

BEDROOMS

The perfect location for your bedroom very much depends on whether you regard yourself to be an emotional sort of person, therefore 'watery', an intellectual, and therefore 'airy', or of a more 'fiery' and excitable nature. A general rule is that too much of anything is likely to harm both constitution and fortune. With this in mind, therefore, it is not a good idea to sleep in the northeastern segment of your home – the area governed by the water element – if you are emotional, as this will only exaggerate the fact. A far better place for a watery person is in the opposite corner of your home, the southwest, where the fire element will provide a balance.

Likewise, a competitive, hot-blooded individual should seek the aetheric northeast, which will serve to calm an all too excitable mind. Incidentally, a fiery person who sleeps in the southwest will experience disturbed sleep patterns and family arguments. Such problems will intensify, should the bed then be in the southwest corner of that room. Similarly, an airy person will only increase a natural restlessness by sleeping in the northwest quarter of the home, governed by the air element, and may suffer from insomnia. The calming influence of the northeast is a much better choice.

A bedroom in the Northwest will increase restlessness no matter how comfortable it may be. It is however an excellent position for a guest room.

THE BED

According to Vastu tradition the framework of a bed should be made of wood, in keeping with the rooms associations with the planet Venus and the natural world. A metal bed should be avoided, primarily because it is not a product of organic growth, but also because metals are associated with the oppressive nature of Saturn and the aggression of Mars.

The bedroom, realm of Venus is also a place for the natural world. Venus is concerned with growing things such as plants and flowers therefore it is preferable to have a wooden bed, a product of nature than a metal bed stead which hint at the natures of gloomy Saturn and aggressive Mars.

Vastu sages believed stipulated that the height of a bed should not exceed one span, equivalent to 40cm (16in), and that the ideal width of a mattress should be 1.3m (4ft) – a convenient measurement because it is roughly equivalent to a standard "queen-sized" mattress. The ideal length of a mattress is given as 2m, (7ft), which is very long by modern Western thinking. An importance is also placed on the presence of a headboard, ideally patterned with flowery or leaf-like motifs.

AN INTRODUCTION TO VASTU

THE POSITION OF THE BED

The bed is undoubtedly the most vital component of the room. It tends to be a large, bulky item of furniture and, in keeping with Vastu tradition, should therefore be positioned in the southwest, west or southern sector. Above all, the bed should not occupy the precise centre of the room because this placement will prevent blessings radiating from the sacred area of the creator-god Brahma. This is also the case for any other large pieces of furniture.

It also equally important for neither the head, nor any side of the bed, to make contact with the wall closest to it. Instead, a distance of at least 10cm (4in) is recommended, so that the *prana*, which tends to hug the boundaries of the room, is able to flow freely. If the bed is too close to the wall it will disturb these energies and may disturb the sleep patterns of the bed's occupant.

Pamper yourself in your bedroom. Breakfast in bed can be a sensual experience.

WARDROBES, CHESTS AND CABINETS

In addition to the bed, most rooms will have any number of other large pieces of furniture, for example, a chest of drawers, a dressing table and a wardrobe. The best positions for such items are in the south, the west and the southwest. There is no problem if the room is large enough to accommodate all of the large furniture in these sectors, but this is not always feasible, and some consideration needs to be made

As usual with heavy furniture, wardrobes should be ideally positioned in the Southwest to prevent nightmares.

for the Vastu need to maintain a visual balance. A good solution is to position the heaviest piece of furniture, the wardrobe, in the south, with the bed in the west, making sure to avoid the exact centre of the room. Lighter furnishings, for example a wicker chair or a small bureau can address the balance in northeast sector, although both the north and east are also permissible.

BEDROOMS

THE SACRED CENTRE

In a small bedroom, it may not be possible to avoid having the bed over the exact centre of the room, thus preventing the creative blessings of Brahma to flow freely. Should this be the case, a symbolic appeasement to Brahma will need to be made, most simply, by making the colour red (the colour identified with the creator-god) a dominant feature of the room's décor. In Vedic tradition, red is the colour of spirituality and possesses the ability to expel evil influences. It is the colour, therefore, of protection and can bestow courage and benevolence.

The fact that the bed occupies the centre of this bedroom is, in Vastu terms an offence to Brahma and the sacred centre. However, a natural appeasement to Brahma has been made in the form of the red bed linen. Red being a colour which pleases the creator-god.

An alternative is to introduce an image of Brahma or of another symbol that represents the concept of benevolent creation. For example, the image of a swan, the creature on which Brahma is sometimes depicted riding, can achieve the same effect. However, if your personal taste does not incline to the Orient, you can use your imagination to achieve a sacred centre within yourself, here, in the most private area of your home.

VENUS AND NATURE IN THE BEDROOM

This area of the home comes under the auspices of the planet Venus and, in Western culture, both this planet and the goddess of the same name are synonymous with love. Venus is also goddess of the natural world and this should be expressed within the intimacy of the bedroom. This can be achieved by introducing a few healthy plants, by choosing wooden furniture in preference to that made of metal and by using cotton rather than acrylic sheets.

The potential harm caused by the metal bed stead is offset by the wooden bedside cabinets. Wood being the product of organic growth is more pleasing to the energies of Venus.

AN INTRODUCTION TO VASTU

There should be an emphasis on beauty and aesthetic appeal in the bedroom, with every item selected to provoke thoughts of love. This is not just a question of physical passions either, since affection for family and friends can be expressed here too. Include photographs of love ones, but remember that if these are of the deceased, the best place for them is in the southwest sector.

Lavender in a container close to the bed, or lavender essence sprinkled on the pillows will relieve anxiety and promote deep sleep.

Keeping some lavender close to the bed will soothe a troubled mind and lead to deep, blissful sleep. If you like candles in this area, the best place for them is in the southwest quadrant, where there is the least risk of fire.

Beautification is part of the glamour of Venus. Try to inject some of that glamour into your own bedroom.

ELECTRICAL EQUIPMENT

The best place for a television or music centre is in the direction of the fire-god Agni, the southeast. If you feel you tend to watch too much television, then the opposite corner, the northwest, is more suitable, as facing this direction will encourage you to lose interest quickly.

Take care not to fall asleep with the television switched. In addition to having a physical presence, humans also possess a strong electro-magnetic field

BEDROOMS

which one might describe as an aura. The continuous pulses of energy from a television set can disrupt this aura during sleep, leading to a lack of rest and consequent depletion of energy on waking. The same applies to having a computer in a bedroom, which should also be switched off during sleep. It is even better if the power to these units is cut completely, since having them on 'standby' only reduces the power output by a third.

Electrical equipment should be switched off before you retire. The standby setting still means that the item is electrically charged.

THE TRANQUILLITY ZONE

Unlike any other room of the house, the entire bedroom should be regarded as a tranquillity zone in its own right. By definition, the bedroom is an intensely private space, reflecting the innermost recesses of one's personality. This is a place to be at one with oneself, an area of safety, and a retreat from the outside world. Remember that this is also the place for love, under the rule of the planet Venus. There should be sense of protection and immediate comfort on entering the room. Its ambience should be soft and inviting so that, when you sleep or make love, you feel the positive vibrations refreshing your soul.

THE MASTER BEDROOM

The guidelines for bedrooms in general also apply to the master bedroom, the sleeping area of the dominant individual in the home. This room is best located in the southwest which, although associated with Nirriti and, by association, nightmares, also has links with notions of responsibility and duty. It is an "earthy" direction, implying dominance over one's surroundings. It is a good idea to sleep in this area if you want to be master or mistress of your own home – especially if you can manage to face north while doing so. The southwest is a *tamas* direction (see page 15) and this 'negative' force increases an inclination for rest, relaxation and inactivity.

Despite the negative reputation of the Southwest it is a good idea to sleep in this area if you want to master or mistress of your home.

AN INTRODUCTION TO VASTU

Romance should be the keynote for the master bedroom. This is the room of the love-goddess Venus and it should reflect the more amorous side to your nature. Bear this fact in mind when thinking about the details. Soft mood lighting, soothing romantic music and beautiful images will lead the mind to thoughts of amour, making this room a temple to your physical and spiritual love.

The zone of tranquillity is extremely important in the master bedroom, particularly if the rest of your home is dominated by boisterous children. Extra care should be taken in following the general guidelines to make this room more inviting, secure and relaxing. A small area set aside for quiet contemplation is a good idea, and should be located as close to the gateway of the gods, in the northeast, as possible.

A CHILD'S BEDROOM

Technically, this room can be located anywhere within the home, but there are certain directions that should be avoided for a peaceful life. For

Including yellow in the décor of a child's room will stimulate the mind and add to the intellectual curiosity. Yellow is also considered a colour which brings positivity an optimism into a child's life.

In Vastu it is considered best if a child's room faces East. However if this is the case then you might consider heavy curtains to prevent your offspring waking up far too early and rousing the house.

BEDROOMS

example, the southwest will encourage offspring to dominate, leaving you feeling like a servant in your own home.

The southeast is a better option, because of the life giving qualities of Agni the fire-god, but may encourage an element of hyperactivity and an adamant refusal to go to bed on time. A teenager who should seek independence might benefit from a bedroom location in the northwest because the 'airy' nature of this direction will promote a questing spirit and ultimately lead to a child taking responsibility for his or her own life. Traditionally the eastern side of your home is the most ideal location for a child's bedroom because of the rays of the rising sun are said to have nurturing qualities. (However, it is wise to consider heavy curtains for the windows in an east-facing room to prevent a child waking too early).

Visual stimulation is important to a young child so items like this mobile should reflect the child's individuality and interests.

SLEEPLESS NIGHTS?

Children who have trouble getting off to sleep or who wake in the night will benefit from having the head of their bed oriented towards the south. This direction seems to have a calming influence on the young, and has the added benefit of bestowing illumination and encouraging the development of maturity.

NURTURING TALENT

Much of a child's life is taken up with learning, not just through formal education, but also by observing the world around them and discovering their place within it. It is important that a child's interests and individuality are reflected in his or her bedroom. This will encourage young people to express their personalities and gifts. A large bulletin board is a good idea, for example for displaying a child's drawings, or showing posters, favourite pop stars and fashionable imagery.

AN INTRODUCTION TO VASTU

A child's room should also be a place of fun. Toys and books should be close together so that learning becomes associated with play. If there is a computer console, it should be located so that the young person faces north while playing games or getting on with homework. This could combine with a tranquillity zone in the northeast corner of the room, which will give the child a sense that he will not be disturbed in his own private space. It is equally beneficial for a child to face east while reading or engaged in lone activities, but facing the west or south could encourage temper tantrums. Vibrant, clashing colours in this room will affect a child's capacity for concentration, and should be avoided.

This airy, sunlit room is ideal for both adults and children to interact.

A child's room should have plenty of activity. It should be "busy" with plenty to stimulate a child's interest. It should be a place of fun with toys and books close together so learning becomes associated with play.

BEDROOMS

THE GUEST BEDROOM

The Spanish and the Japanese share a proverb along the lines 'visitors and fish go off after three days' and, although hospitality is a great virtue, it is unpleasant to house lodgers who show no signs of a readiness to leave.

Guest bedrooms should ideally be located in the North-western segment of your home.

This room should be more personalised. The guest room is not in a hotel, it is part of your home.

For this reason Vastu guidelines recommend that a guest bedroom should be located in the northwest of the home – an area governed by the regent Vayu and the restless element of air. This sector should ensure that, after a short period, your beloved and welcome guests will feel the need to move on. If you want your guests to stay for a prolonged period this room is best in different area of the home. Avoid the southwest, however, as, over a period of time, the house starts to feel more theirs than one's own.

The guest bedroom should never be a neutral space, but should express the personalities of yourself and your family. Photographs of loved ones or pictures reflecting personal interests should feature here. These will reinforce the face that this room is part of your home and is only a temporary base for your guest.

Any items which reflect your interests are good features in the guest room.

THE BATHROOM

THROUGHOUT THE INDIAN sub-continent, and indeed wherever Hindu faith is practised, the act of taking a bath has a deep ritual significance. Therefore, in Vastu tradition, the bathroom is an extremely important area, imbued with holiness. It is here that the physical body, the very envelope of the soul, is cleansed. And, since body and soul are so intertwined in Hindu belief, the inner self is also renewed and made pure.

Of course, in previous centuries the only buildings with any type of bathroom were mansions and palaces, where the ornate washing facilities tended to be associated with a harem and located in the southwest of the home, within easy reach of the master bedroom. More humble dwellings did not possess a bathroom at all.

THE TEMPLE OF BODY AND SPIRIT

In classical Vastu terms, when we think 'bathroom' we should also think 'temple', for this is a private, sacred space – an inner holy of holies within the confines of the home. The bathroom, above all other rooms in the house, should reflect the personalities of the occupants of the home and the wonders of the natural world while providing a secure and comfortable environment.

Modern emphasis on hygiene fits well with the ancient Vastu precepts. The Victorian adage 'cleanliness is next to godliness' might just as well have been spoken

The bathroom is the temple of the body and spirit. It should be a place of purification both of the physical self and of the soul. In Vastu terms "cleanliness is next to godliness". The bathroom should not be used as a quick convenience. It is a place to linger and pamper oneself.

THE BATHROOM

by one of the great Vastu sages, who emphasise the importance of using only natural products in the bathroom and on the body.

A long lingering bath should become a pleasurable habit in a Vastu bathroom.

The perfect Vastu bathroom is not a place to be used as a quick convenience. Its function should not be misused by racing in for a swift shower or merely to brush one's teeth. The ambience of the room should be such that one wishes to linger, to relax, to take long, lingering baths, to pamper oneself and to achieve a sense of calm security. Time should be taken to allow the mind to wander while bathing. This invigorating watery area of the home should reinforce positive mental attitudes during the cleansing of the physical form. The vastu bathroom is as much a place for the spirit as it is for the body.

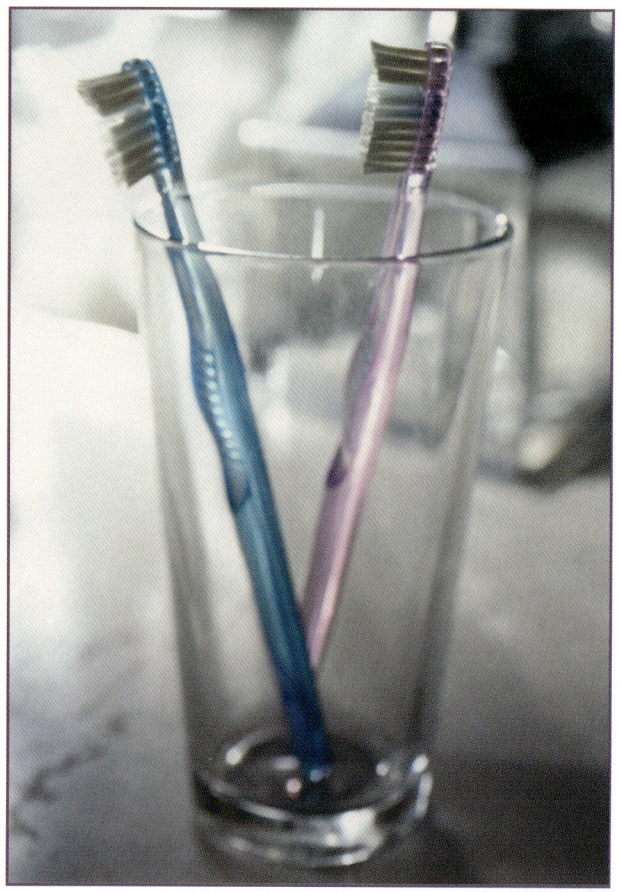

Don't just rush into the bathroom to brush your teeth, linger a while.

THE REJUVENATING POWER OF SOMA

In Indian belief, the god Soma is the moon-god. He is either considered to be a personification of the elixir of life or the deity who brews it. Either way, it is from Soma that physical wellbeing stems. Soma is a watery deity, ruler of the tides, and subject to change. His direction, the northeast, is the fount of all goodness, and he has particular significance in the bathroom.

The ancient epic Hindu text the *Mayamata* speaks of the place of Soma thus 'The bathroom should be rendered beautiful, free from dirt and hair, and filled with flowers, plants and fragrant substances.' It goes on to advise that white robes should be worn after bathing (in honour of the moon) preferably made of silk.

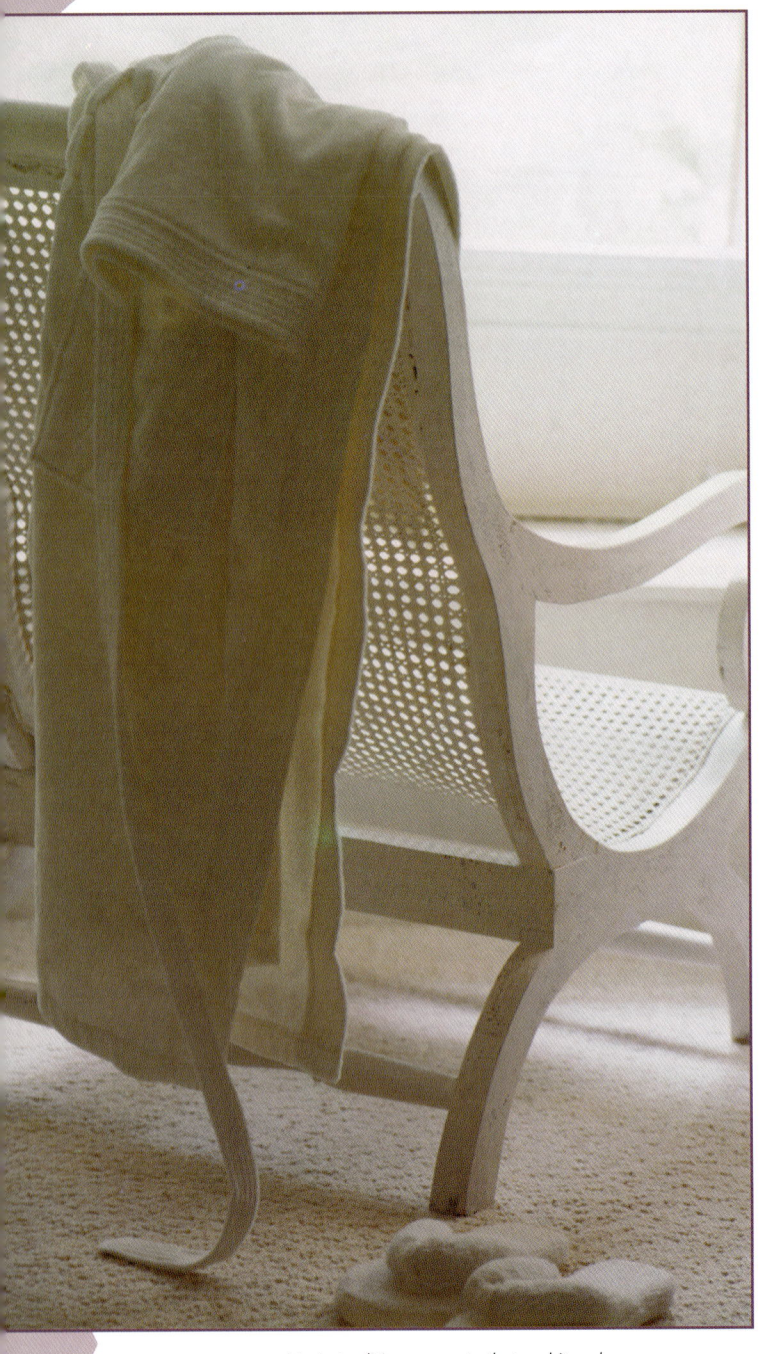

AN INTRODUCTION TO VASTU

Vastu tradition suggests that a white robe (in honour of the moon) be worn after bathing.

The regent Soma ruler of the Northeast is symbolised by reflective surfaces, especially mirrors. This round mirror is particularly apt since it not only expressed lunar influences but also is round, the symbolic shape associated with the water element.

The regent Soma is also symbolised by reflective surfaces, and most especially by mirrors. Mirrors are a necessity in a bathroom and should be placed along the northern and eastern walls.

THE NATURAL WORLD

Plants and flowers are energising, filled with life force so their inclusion in a bathroom is fitting. In fact, there are various aspects of nature that can be introduced to achieve a state of a calm contemplation within a bathroom. Choose restful landscapes or seascapes to represent the awesome power of the living world, or try images of fish, dolphins or seahorses. Shells and other sea ornaments are also appropriate.

THE BATHROOM

Items suggestive of water or the sea are recommended here. These sea-shells fit the Vastu bill completely.

Ornaments of silver and blue in shapes suggestive of water are always a good feature in a bathroom.

As ever nature should be allowed some space. If there is enough natural light in your bathroom then a healthy plant that likes a steamy atmosphere would be a welcome addition to your decor.

LOCATION, LOCATION, LOCATION

By definition the bathroom is a watery area of the home, yet it may seem surprising that it is not recommended to have the bathroom in the watery northeast. This quarter is the gateway of the gods and is not suitable for bulky items here such as bathtubs and shower units, which may block the flow of *prana*. Quite apart from that, having a bathroom here would produce an overabundance of water, in turn leading to hidden undercurrents of emotion within the family.

101

AN INTRODUCTION TO VASTU

En-suite facilities are an unwelcome development as far as Vastu is concerned.

Traditionally the southwest was the preferred location for a bathroom, but the northwest is equally acceptable, although it may encourage restlessness. By far the best location for the bathroom is in the eastern, where the early light of the sun can bathe the room in the glory of Indra, the ever-youthful king of the Vedic gods. This is especially true if your bathroom and toilet are in separate areas.

EN-SUITE FACILITIES

The concept of an *en-suite* bathroom is a modern innovation and, in Vastu terms, is an unwelcome development because bedroom and bathroom have radically different functions and their symbolic resonance is quite distinct from each other. One way to reduce the damage that an en-suite bathroom can do to your fortunes and peace of mind is to keep the connecting door closed at all times.

THE TOILET

There are few rules in Vastu concerning the toilet itself, which should not be broken if good fortune is to enter your home. The first rule is that, for reasons of hygiene, the toilet should not be too close to the kitchen. The second rule is more of a recommendation that the toilet should the oriented along the *agni-rekha* or fire line running north-south (see page 9). Furthermore, the toilet should be sited so that one faces north when seated.

THE TRANQUILLITY ZONE

The best possible zone of serenity in a bathroom is the bath itself. This is a place of peace, of contemplation and of positive thinking. Where better to linger, than a bathtub, to think good thoughts and allow the

The best possibly tranquillity zone is the bath itself.

THE BATHROOM

tensions of the day to soak away. Uniquely, in Vastu tradition, this specific tranquillity zone should not be in the northeast quadrant of the bathroom, which would invite unruly emotions into your home and family life.

Soak away your tensions with a lingering, softly scented bath.

DÉCOR AND LIGHTING

Vastu recommends that the décor of the bathroom should reflect the influence of the sea or of the moon. Soft greens and blues are perfect colours for this area, as is white. If a modern look is preferred, a white tiled bathroom with modest features of green and blue, such as bath mats, towels and small ornaments is perfect. Chrome fittings and mirrors (on the northern or eastern walls only) would also add to the overall effect. It is good Vastu practice to have subdued lighting in the bathroom in order to create an under-water ambience. Candlelight is ideal, as long as care is taken.

Personalise your bathroom space with attractive ornaments and details.

The colours of the bathroom should reflect those of the sea or of the moon.

The shining, reflective chrome sink is reminiscent of the moon.

THE HOME OFFICE

THESE DAYS MANY people own a personal computer, and are busy 'surfing the net' for much of their leisure time. Many home computers as used for work as well as pleasure so it is becoming increasingly common for a room to be set aside as a home office or study. The result is that many of us spend as much time in the home office as we do in the living room or bedroom.

As with other rooms in the home, furniture placement and décor need careful attention, a tranquillity zone is vital and one must ensure that nothing in the ambience of the room is distracting or negative, as this will have a profound effect on your chances of business success. This space should be positive, uplifting and a joy to be in. It should suit your personality and reflect your own tastes. This is particularly true if you are the only person in the household to use the office. The same guidelines apply if you don't work from home as such, but do have an area in which you write correspondence or play games on a computer.

A good colour to choose for this room is yellow because this primary is associated with the cleverness of Mercury or Budha and will stimulate the mind, providing clarity of thought.

THE DANGERS OF CLUTTER

An aura of peace is vital in this area of your home and will prevent a tendency to allow work to rule one's life. It is necessary to create a space in which concentration and application are enhanced, but is a bad idea to think of the home office simply as a place of duty and drudgery. To this end it is important that the room is kept clean and uncluttered. Clearing up work clutter is always a challenge, especially when one is busy, but time should be made for this task. Indeed, the very act of tidying up can be a mentally clarifying experience. Clutter, and in particular, piles of paper that are left for

It is becoming increasingly common for part of a room to be set up as a computer station or home office. The home office should be psychologically separated from the rest of the room. A good colour for this area is yellow which stimulates the mind and makes one intellectually active.

THE HOME OFFICE

Clutter left for long periods will become a reservoir of negative energy.

thankless tasks. To avoid these symptoms of an unhappy working life and to create lots of positive mental energy, ensure that your work space is organised to optimum efficiency with a place for everything, and everything in its place!

long periods become reservoirs of stagnant negative energy. People who work in an environment that is disorganised and untidy will soon lose their focus and may become depressed. A messy workspace is associated with the grim planet Saturn or Shani, the celestial governor of despondency, hopelessness and

Remember to keep everything in its place.

Try to organise yourself into having a place for everything.

It is easy to have too much furniture in a home office, particularly if the room in question is doubling up as an occasional bedroom. With a little imagination and, perhaps, minor expense, however, you can transform a messy environment into one that is adaptable and tasteful at the same time. A fold-down sofa bed or Japanese-style futon chair is an ideal piece of furniture for such a room.

AN INTRODUCTION TO VASTU

This cat seems to have found her own zone of tranquillity.

LOCATION, LOCATION, LOCATION

Since the home office is such an important area to a wide variety of people, there are three ideal locations for it. The west is associated with communications. This is a good place for a study if you spend hours on the phone, or if you are constantly e-mailing your clients or colleagues. The east is good if you are involved in creative ventures. Both directions are good for writers, who tend to be both creative and communicative. Of course the north, the direction of prosperous Kubera and genial Jupiter, is also a good location for an office because this placement promises an increased chance of business success. The north is particularly good if you are involved in intense study or research.

THE HOME OFFICE

The North is the best direction in which to keep valued books.

ARRANGING THE FURNITURE

Basic furniture for a home office consists of a desk, shelving units and probably a filing cabinet or two. These items are the essentials, but there is no reason why a couple of chairs or a comfortable sofa cannot be included also, if space allows.

It's a pity that so few of us could successfully live in such a minimalist environment.

The south, the area of death and the afterlife, should be avoided at all costs, and the ill-omened southwest is associated with bad luck. The northwest, while not unfortunate in itself, will nevertheless prove too airy and distracting for prolonged periods of concentration, while the watery northeast – usually so beneficial – is too unworldly and meditative for practical affairs. However, if the room doubles up as a bedroom, then the northeast of the room is precisely the place for your desk while the opposite corner, the southwest is a good place for the bed. The southeast, the direction of the fire-god Agni, is better suited to more physical activities. Anything too mentally taxing will soon lead to boredom and a lack of focus.

The more bulky items of furniture, for example filing cabinets, bookcases, beds and sofas, should be located in the southwest. If a bookcase will fit into an alcove so much the better, otherwise it is important that all items of furniture have at least 10cm (4in) between them and the wall.

AN INTRODUCTION TO VASTU

Electrical equipment can be placed in the fiery sector of the southeast. This includes computers and music centres but not a television. It is unwise to include a television in this room because it will prove to be extremely distracting. If there has to be a set in this room, place it in the northwest corner so that you can turn it off easily.

The important item of furniture in the home office is obviously the desk, ideally sited in the west or the south (preferably the latter if particularly heavy). The south also has the benefit of bestowing decisiveness, leadership qualities and inner strength on the occupants of the room. If your desk is in the south you should sit facing north – the direction of wealth and wellbeing. A western location for the desk is good for those who are involved in mass communications and creative work. Sit facing east to encourage inspiration, concentration and the ability to focus on the job at hand.

Be aware that, despite offering calmness and serenity, facing northeast has its perils. By facing northeast you are sitting in the ill-omened southwest and this will invite bad luck. This seating position is only permissible if you have something large and heavy behind you, such as a bulky cabinet or bookshelves, to provide the necessary barriers against the regent Nirriti, goddess of nightmares.

THE TRANQUILLITY ZONE

An area of serenity and calm is very important in a working environment, where every effort should be made to relieve stress and work pressure. Fortunately, the tranquillity zone in an office space need not be large or too overt. The best directions for this

The desk, or in this case, the drawing-board is ideally located in the West.

If your office space allows a lightweight chair can be placed in your tranquillity zone.

THE HOME OFFICE

If space allows, a wicker or other lightweight chair can be placed in the tranquillity zone, where you can sit and ponder. If the room is too small, you can make a symbolic gesture to the concept of serenity instead. For example, traditional Vastu thinkers might place a small statuette of their favourite deity in this area to provide comfort and inspiration (often the beautiful goddess Lakshmi, bestower of good fortune, or of elephant headed Ganesha, the god of wisdom). We in the Western world may prefer a picture of a beautiful scene (a seascape is recommended in the watery northeast) or some items of sentimental value. The object of this exercise is to give you something to reflect upon when you pause from your labours.

Even though it is an electrical item, place a fan in the airy Northwest of your office to encourage intellectual activity.

The unobtrusive inclusion of boats on the windowsill appeases the watery nature of the Northwest.

meditative area are the inspirational east, the healthful north or the divinely relaxing northeast. The northeast is a particularly good spot for natural elements such as plants, an aquarium or a small indoor fountain.

INDEX

A
Adam, biblical 41
Agni 22, 39-40, 53, 71, 83, 92, 95, 107
Agni-rehka (see also Fire-line) 8, 102
Appeasements 51-59
Aries 52

B
Brahma 9, 16, 17, 44, 57, 67, 90, 91
Budha (see also Mercury) 32-33, 72, 104

C
Capricorn 42
Chandra (see also the Moon) 31-32
Chi 6, 18
China 6
Cosmic Square 8, 10, 11, 12

E
Elements, the five (see also Maha Bhutas) 20
- Aether 20-21
- Air 21-22
- Earth 24-25
- Fire 22-23
- Water 23-24

F
Feng shui 6, 18, 20, 24
Fire-line (see also agni-rehka) 8, 102

G
Ganesha 63, 87, 109
Gemini 53, 58
Guna 14, 15
Guru (see also Jupiter) 35-36, 69

H
Home demon (see also Purusha) 12

I
Indra 38-39, 52, 84, 102

J
Jupiter (see also Guru) 35, 38, 69, 78, 106

K
Ketu 37
Kubera 44, 56, 59, 69, 78, 106
Kuja (see also Mars) 34-35, 83

L
Lakshmi 59, 63, 109

INDEX

M
Maha Bhutas (see also Elements, the five) 20
Mayamata 99,
Mars (see also Kuja) 34-35, 53, 83, 89
Mercury (see also Budha) 32-33, 50, 55, 68, 72, 104
Moon (see also Chandra) 31-32

N
Nirriti 24, 41-42, 54, 55, 61, 72, 84, 93, 108

P
Planets 29-30, 50
the shadow (see also Ketu and Rahu) 37
Prana 7, 18, 19, 56, 57, 60, 62, 69, 83
Purusha (see also home demon) 12, 13, 21, 62

R
Rahu 37
Rajas 15, 18
Regents of Space 7, 38, 48

S
Sacred centre 11
Sattva 14, 16, 18
Saturn (see also Shani) 36-37, 54, 55, 61, 89, 105
Shani (see also Saturn) 36-37, 105
Shiva 16
Shukra (see also Venus) 33-34, 88
Soma 21, 44, 56, 69, 83, 99-100
Sun (see also Surya) 30-31
Surya (see also the Sun) 30-31, 84

T
Tamas 15, 18, 61, 93
Taurus 52
Temple, Hindu 7
Tranquility, zone of 50, 74-75, 81, 87, 93, 108-109
Triguna 14
- square of 17, 61
Trimurti 16

V
Varuna 42, 55
Vayu 21, 22, 23, 43, 55, 68, 97
Vedas 7
Vedic diagram 11, 12, 13, 19
Venus (see also Shukra) 33-34, 52, 54, 88, 89, 91, 93, 94
Vishnu 16, 17, 81

W
Water-line 8
Wind-line 9

Y
Yama 41, 54, 66

Z
Zodiac, 26-28, 49

BIBLIOGRAPHY & CREDITS

BIBLIOGRAPHY

Vastu Shastra	Caroline Robertson	Lansdowne	2001
Vastu Living	Kathleen Cox	Marlowe &Company	2000
Vastu Vidya	Juliet Pegrum	Gaia Books Ltd	2000
The Circle of Stars	Valerie J. Roebuck	Element	1992
Indian Astrology	Ronnie Gale Dreyer	Aquarian	1990
Hindu Astrology	Shil Ponde	Sagar Publications	1975
Feng Shui from Scratch	Jonathan Dee	D&S Books	2001

PICTURE CREDITS

© Stockbyte pp 8 tr, 9tl, 14, 15, 16tl, 18tr, 18br, 19tl, 20, 22, 23bl, 23tr, 25l, 31b, 32l, 33t, 34l, 35, 36b, 39, 40, 42tr, 43r, 44r, 54l, 57tr, 59tr, 60r, 61t, 62tl, 63tr, 69l, 70bl, 70tr, 72bl, 73tl, 75tl, 75r, 76r, 79b, 80tl, 93l, 105tl, 105r,

© Photodisk pp 6, 7, 8l, 9br, 11bl, 12, 13, 16bl, 18l, 19bl, 21l, 21br, 23tl, 23br, 24, 30, 31tr, 32tr, 33b, 43l, 41, 50, 51, 53br, 56tl, 61b, 62tr, 62b, 63br, 64t, 64bl, 66r, 67l, 68bl, 68r, 70t, 70br, 72tl, 74tr, 75bl, 77l, 80b, 81l, 81tr, 82l, 83r, 84r, 85l, 85br, 86t, 88r, 89l, 90, 92, 93r, 96r, 97, 99r, 100l, 102, 103, 105bl, 106, 107, 108, 109l

© David King, p8 br

(where b = bottom, t = top, l = left, r = right)

Acknowledgements

The author and publishers would like to thank Tina, Steve, Olivia & James for kindly allowing their house to be photographed for this book.